M000224206

Pursuing Hope

The Story of Justin Hanna

By

Vanessa E. Hanna-Verrett

Watersprings
PUBLISHING

Pursuing Hope: The Story of Justin Hanna
Published by Watersprings Publishing, a division of
Watersprings Media House, LLC.
P.O. Box 1284
Olive Branch, MS 38654
www.waterspringsmedia.com
Contact publisher for bulk orders and permission requests.

Copyright © 2020 Vanessa E. Hanna-Verrett

All rights reserved. No part of this publication may be reproduced, distributed, or transmitted in any form or by any means, including photocopying, recording, or other electronic or mechanical methods, without the prior written permission of the publisher, except in the case of brief quotations embodied in critical reviews and certain other noncommercial uses permitted by copyright law.

Scripture quotations credited to NIV are from the Holy Bible, New International Version. Copyright © 1973, 1978, 1984, 2011 by Biblica, Inc. Used by permission. All rights reserved worldwide.

Scripture quotations marked "ESV" are taken from The Holy Bible, English Standard Version. Copyright © 2000; 2001 by Crossway Bibles, a division of Good News Publishers. Used by permission. All rights reserved.

Printed in the United States of America.

Library of Congress Control Number: 2020923614

ISBN-13: 978-1-948877-69-5

Table of Contents

Dedication

This book is dedicated to God; to my loving and courageous son, Donavan; to my adoring, nurturing and supportive husband, Leon; to those who feel that persevering through life challenges is hopeless; to those who have experienced the pain of losing someone you love; and especially to parents who have been separated from their children through death. My heart deeply cries with you, desires to encourage you, and prays for you.

Acknowledgments

First of all, I thank God for His patience with me and His unwavering love. Next, I thank my husband, who never met Justin but has been willing to get to know him through my stories and the stories of others. I thank him for his gentle love and for giving me his shoulder to cry on over and over again. I would be utterly remiss not to thank my son Donavan for his love, his courage, his support, for sharing his writing skills, and for being a loving big brother. Also, I want to thank my family, friends, Justin's friends, and all those who made contributions.

Foreword

By Danielle Mounter Byrd

Word started to spread across the campus of Oakwood University that a student had drowned in an accident at the rock quarry. I immediately felt a lump in my throat and an ache in my chest that was becoming all too familiar. Another induction had occurred.

My own induction occurred when I lost my firstborn in a car accident when she was only 4 ½ months old. I had been painfully thrust into lifelong membership of a club that no mother ever wants to join, regardless of the age of their "baby" — the club of mothers who have lost a child. Once a member, however, we are forever bonded to one another by our tears, sleepless nights, and shattered dreams; by a pain only we know and understand. I felt such sorrow knowing that another mother had entered our ranks.

As news of the accident spread to local news channels and plans for a memorial service were being shared, I had a strong desire to reach out to this grieving mother. I wanted to let her know that, although it seemed unimaginable at the time, God would heal her broken heart. I wanted to assure her that there would eventually be a day that was not filled with tears if she could just cling to the promise that God restores. I wanted her to know that she would laugh again, pray again, praise again, and in time, she would trust God again. I wanted to share so many things that I had learned along my personal journey, but I knew her aching heart was not ready to receive any of these sentiments. I prayed that God would wrap her in His arms of comfort and carry her through this time of overwhelming grief.

A few weeks later, I was gathering my belongings after church when an usher approached me and said, "There is a lady in the back of the church that would like to speak with you." I was busily rounding up my daughters along with a group of college students that I had invited over for dinner, when the usher continued, "Her name is Vanessa Hanna. Her son is the student that drowned at the rock quarry."

I stopped in my tracks. I asked the students to wait, and followed the usher to the rear of the sanctuary. As I walked the long aisle to the rear of the church, I asked God to give me the right words to say to this grieving mother, but the moment our eyes met, no words came, only tears. We embraced, and as we clung to each other with tears streaming down our faces, it was clear that no words were necessary. In that moment, a lifelong sisterhood was born out of tragedy.

Pursuing Hope: The Story of Justin Hanna gives insight into the journey through life after unimaginable loss. As you read this mother's heart-wrenching story, you will come to understand how God has used Vanessa's most difficult life experience to encourage others. It is a testimony that will inspire women across the globe who have unexpectedly found themselves inducted into "the club." This book will also prove inspirational for family and friends who desire to support their loved ones during their journey from grief to healing.

Preface

*T*his is not an ordinary book about loss and grief. It is also a story that reflects a loving relationship between a mother and her baby son who passed away on March 23, 2012, at the Rock Quarry in Huntsville, Alabama while attending Oakwood University in his freshman year of college. His name was Justin Emanuel Hanna.

The reality of this book being completed was questioned by me on numerous occasions as I recalled the loss of my youngest son. The intensity and emotional drain of reflecting upon the details was sometimes overwhelming. It was during these periods that I was seeking a word from God to answer my teary-eyed question: "Is this really what I'm supposed to be doing? Writing a book about losing my baby, Justin?" The Holy Spirit revealed the answer over and over again with a clear, calm assurance that my story must be written and shared with others.

This book is needed for the completion of my own healing, as well as to encourage others, and address issues when parents experience the loss of a child. I have come to know after losing my baby that this ordeal could either cause me to withdraw or to be transparent in order to help others.

Ultimately, this story must be shared to help the wounded, the sorrowful, and those who may be in denial to learn to let go and let God; to learn that God is not the enemy but the ultimate source of healing.

It is my desire for *Pursuing Hope: The Story of Justin Emanuel Hanna* to be a platform to help lead others to Christ and restore broken relationships with Him.

To God be the glory,
Vanessa E. Hanna-Verrett, Mother

Chapter 1

The Awaited Moment: The Making of Justin Emanuel Hanna

W ouldn't you agree that anticipation is a beautiful thing? It had been five years since Donavan, our first bundle of joy was born, and now we were anticipating our second bundle of joy. I mused, *surely this is going to be easier the second time than it was the first time — it was soon pretty evident that I did not completely know what I was talking about.* Just as every child is different, every pregnancy is different too.

I remember during my second trimester, I was torn about whether I wanted to know our baby's gender before giving birth. I just couldn't decide and appreciated the nurse's patience and participation. These were my instructions to the nurse at the doctor's office: "Write down if the baby is a boy or a girl; then, I will decide if I really want to know the result or not."

As I reflect on that period and my personality, I realize I was and am the type of person who is easily excited and ever wondering, even when the topic is something far less life-changing than having a baby.

If the opportunity presented itself, the part of Alice in the story of *Alice in Wonderland* could easily and effectively be played by me. Why? Because, just like Alice, I become "curiouser and curiouser". I soon had to grasp the reality that I was entirely too excited about my baby's arrival to avoid looking at that piece of paper, which revealed: It was a boy!

There were a couple of things, though, that I was not excited about. The first was that my body was now five years older, and as my pregnancy progressed, it felt 10 years older. Oh, my goodness! My hormone levels were different than what I experienced previously, and my fatigue levels were higher. Also, with my first pregnancy, I worked up to my delivery date. However, this time, I was ready to stop working at least a month before my due date.

Nevertheless, my doctor was not of the same mindset, recommending that I just keep working for as long as I could. That was not what I wanted to hear because the heat was both excessive and draining during July, the hottest month of the year. Imagine this: I look like I'm carrying a gigantic basketball, and my body feels like it's being stretched beyond its limits. Any woman that has ever been pregnant can likely relate to what I'm describing.

The second thing that I was not excited about was the fact that Don and I could not agree on a name for our baby. However, I was destined to waddle along for a little while longer and try to be as positive as possible.

As I was processing the changes taking place in my body and trying to maintain a healthy attitude, I also began to think about the strong black women in my family. The strength that I am referring to is physical and mental. Some of them have gone to sleep, such as my mother and grandmothers, but others are still carving out their legacies. In my opinion, regardless of race, creed, or color, it takes a strong woman to willfully have more than two babies. I admire those of you who do! My mom had four of us while my maternal grandmother had five, and my paternal grandmother had a whopping 14 children. *Wow!* Nevertheless, two children were all I wanted at that point (June 1993), and Don agreed.

Later in my life, I would learn the extent of my strength. At this particular time, the pressing matter at hand was that our baby did not yet have a name, and we were running out of time. The idea of a birth certificate that reads "Baby Hanna" was not helping my hormonal state, but I was excited about welcoming my dear baby to our family.

Our family members were also getting concerned, and some of them were concerned to the point of beginning to select names for us! Donavan wanted his little brother to be named "David" since that was his favorite Bible character, and he also liked "Joshua." I really wanted to appease my son and have him feel a part of the process, but I wasn't fond of the name "David," though the name "Joshua" could be given some consideration. Those were the good suggestions; you should have heard some of the other names. Yikes! One thing we could agree on was that it needed to be something that could easily be spelled!

The name saga continued. Don's legal name is Silvaris Hanna. Our first child's full name is Silvaris Donavan Hanna. He wanted to name our second child "Silvaris Hanna." Keep in mind that my hormone levels were naturally out of sync. I was getting close to 40 weeks in my pregnancy, it was 100 degrees and smoking hot in Florence, South Carolina, and we were at a stand-still about our name. My husband's family name is Don (a different story). So, I said, "Don, we are not following in George Foreman's footsteps with this. We are not naming all of our children the same name." Naming Donavan was far less challenging than this time around. This naming process was somewhat complex and almost hysterically funny.

Obviously, after much discussion, there were several other names discussed. Praise the Lord! My husband was giving consideration to some other names. One of the names that he liked was Stephan. However, the name that we all finally came to an agreement on was Justin, which is a Latin word meaning "just, upright, righteous." His middle name would be Emanuel, which means "God with us" and is my maiden name. Yes! Our baby boy would be called Justin Emanuel Hanna.

A couple of weeks passed, and my sonogram showed a healthy baby and mother. Thank God! As we got closer to the due date, which was now just days away, Justin was nicely positioned, and the dilation process had begun. I was exhausted and growing exponentially ready for this little one to make his appearance. As a mother, you know how intense labor pains can be, and as soon as a hard labor pain hit, my message changed to "Oh Lord! I'm not ready yet!" Pregnancy is both beautiful and disturbingly scary at the same time.

Finally, after seven hours of labor, the awaited moment was here! Don's eyes displayed so much joy as he held him in his arms. It was Saturday, July 31, 1993 at 7 a.m., and Justin Emanuel Hanna had arrived to make his mark on the world. Thank You, God!

"Give thanks to the Lord, for he is good!" (Psalm 118:1, NLT)

Chapter 2

The New Norm

Whenever a baby enters your life, there is always an adjustment period, no matter how well you feel you have prepared. The next day, I woke up with joy in my heart because we were bringing our little baby, Justin Emanuel Hanna, home. Donavan had been at the hospital all night with us and was just as excited as we were. He just smiled at his little brother and never displayed any signs of jealousy toward him. He loved him from the very beginning and was very protective. Donavan displayed qualities of a nurturing big brother, and Justin was a sweet little baby. Our family was now complete because the special number for us was two. Now it is time to focus on making sure we take good care of these little boys we love so much.

Throughout the course of enjoying this time at home with our sons, I knew a time would come when I would have to leave them to return to work. Naturally, I was very thankful for my job, but I wasn't ready to leave Donavan nor Justin at such an early stage. I realized that the formative years were crucial for bonding and other reasons, and I was not ready to let go. Every day, I thanked God for our families because they were a great source of support and strength for Don and I. It seemed that as quickly as maternity leave began, it came to an end. We knew that the support of family would be crucial.

My maternal grandmother, Isabelle Smith, was our initial babysitter for both of our sons. It was a perfect set-up since she lived in close proximity to our home and truly enjoyed spending time with her great-grandsons. My parents and in-laws also provided support and love for our children throughout the years. As I reflect back, we could have raised our children alone, but it was so much better for us and our sons to have that family connection and support. It brought Don and I a great deal of comfort to have those around us that we could trust to care for Donavan and Justin. It really does take a village to raise a child; that famous old African proverb meant more to us than just a slogan. It was important for us to continue to maintain the family structure as our sons grew older.

We all know that babies do not remain small for very long. As a parent, it is so remarkable how one minute we are holding their tiny little bodies in our arms, studying every aspect of their face, counting their fingers and toes, and observing them intensely to make sure that our precious little ones are healthy and well-nurtured. It seems the next moment they are crawling around in wonder of their new world and abilities. It was my experience that pots and pans never made so much noise as they did in the hands of a toddler, and Justin was no exception. As Justin began exploring, his actions seemed to say, "If I concentrate and become really determined, I can surely get from one point to another a little bit faster." He was not quite as active as Donavan was, but still, keeping up with him was enough to get my heart rate elevated.

Justin was inquisitive and very adept at applying small and large motor skills. I remember watching him take his first steps at 10 months old and the times of holding his little fingers while walking and exploring the world around him. We were happy and proud of his accomplishments. His explorative abilities surpassed his stature, and as he became sturdier, he began walking along the back of the sofa, which was more than a bit frightening! My little boy remained tiny in height and width for what seemed like a very long time, and as parents, we had accepted the notion that he was going to be short like Grandma Essie and Grandma Dot. However, his height had no impact on the growth of his personality.

He had always been his own person, and as Justin grew and developed, it became more obvious that he would wear his own unique personality and would be quite comfortable with who he was becoming. Now, sometimes that would be a blessing, and other times, it would produce an opportunity for parental counseling.

What do I mean by that? Let me share a few stories with you.

When this tiny toddler was about 2 years old, his Auntie Nette purchased him some clothes which we thought were cute and adorable. There were about six of us in the room encouraging Justin to like the clothes as much as we did.

Auntie said, "Look, Justin. Do you like what Auntie bought for you?"

With shocking clarity and crisp intonation, my tiny toddler spoke with more absoluteness than I wanted him to possess at that moment.

He opened his mouth and said, "I don't yike it, and I don't want it!" We were astonished and embarrassed because he had never expressed himself in that manner before.

As you can imagine, the room was eerily silent. It was like, by reason of some strange phenomenon, we all became mute simultaneously. You should have seen the bewildered, shocked expressions on our faces. We turned to look at Auntie Nette, whose feelings were obviously crushed, and then looked away.

Fortunately, time can be a wonderful healer, and this starburst of revealed personality became a family joke that we laugh about until this day. By the way, Justin and Auntie Nette developed a special relationship, and he received many more gifts over the years.

Another time, when he was about 3 years old, his Grandma Dot was having a discussion with him, and apparently, it was something that he was not in favor of based on the stomping of his little foot, which seemed like it was only an inch long. Grandma had a special, firm-but-loving talk with him, and fortunately, that incident never repeated itself.

Then, when Justin was 4, he and Donavan were visiting with my parents, Grandma Essie and Grandaddy Son. Grandma Essie could be described as mellow, soft-spoken, kind, and nurturing. Grandaddy Son could be described as protective, a provider, caring but moody, with a no-nonsense, Type-A personality, sprinkled with an unpredictable sense of humor. It was no surprise that on this particular day, Granddaddy was having a solemn moment, and everyone knew not to disturb him. These were the times we tried to have as little interaction as possible. He walked into the house and went directly over to his granddad, looked up into his face, and simply said "Hey, Granddaddy!" That was all it took to break the solemnity and bring a smile to his grandfather's face.

My mother privately shared this story with me and added, "Justin knows how to get to his Granddaddy." Here he demonstrated discernment and compassion toward his grandfather. He could have shied away from the situation but instead, approached it in his own way; little did I know that this trait would continue throughout his life.

Don and I often asked ourselves, "When did he start saying that?" "When did he start doing that?" or saying, "I cannot believe that my baby is starting kindergarten!" Time did not stop for us, and that was all the more evident as we watched our children grow and develop right in front of us.

> *"There's an opportune time to do things, a right time for everything on the earth."* (Ecclesiastes 3:1, MSG)

Chapter 3

School and All of Its Wonders

mazingly, Grandma Bella was already in her 90s when she took on the role of a nurturing babysitter for Justin. As you can imagine, to be even considered for a babysitter, she was quite agile for her age. She enjoyed the blessings of being in excellent physical and mental health and even still drove her blue Buick. However, because of the continuous and consistent care a young child requires, we knew that her love and desire to help would outlast her physical stamina. We were very grateful that one and a half years passed before that day became a reality. It was time for Justin to migrate from his sheltered life into a daycare environment. Even though he would be attending a church-affiliated daycare, it was still an emotional transition for me as well.

There were numerous questions circling around in my mind as I wondered how my baby would adjust to his new school life. Many working parents, especially mothers, can identify with the flood of emotions and questions that come when sending our children off to school for the first time. Some of my questions included, "How will he and the other children interact?" "How will he adjust to the teacher's style of teaching, or will she be exceptional and adjust to his?" "Will he be treated fairly?" "Will Christ truly be demonstrated in daily interactions with the teacher?"

Ironically, it was my concern about this transition that helped me to reflect inwardly and remember that being concerned about your child's well-being is natural for loving parents, and being anxious and worried would not make the situation better — potentially worse. Along with trusting in God, it is our job as parents to research where our children will be taught because faith without works is dead, and God's job as our loving Father is to work things out on our behalf according to His wisdom and His will. The Bible tells us in 1 Thessalonians 5:17 (KJV) to *"pray without ceasing"* and Psalm 62:8 (NIV) tells us to *"pour out your hearts to Him, for God is our refuge."* As Christian parents, we kept our children continuously before the Lord, and that was my commitment as we prepared for kindergarten.

The first day of kindergarten came, and Justin looked so cute in his little pants and matching shirt. I was still not completely sure how he was going to react when I left him there though. Many of us have witnessed some children having a very traumatic experience, as they are seen crying, kicking, and screaming, and my heart goes out to those parents and children when I see them today. As parents, Don and I, along with other family members, were hoping and praying that he would have a positive experience. The amazing thing to me was that Justin was embracing these changes very calmly. Although I was careful to not allow my emotions to show outwardly, it seemed that Justin processed this transition better than I did.

He was very calm as we took that long walk from the parking lot to the front door of the school; with optimism but without full recognition of the fact, he not only walked into a building but into a new chapter of his life. I could actually expel a sigh of relief when he did not shed one tear; having said that, if he had followed me back to the car, he could very well have seen multiple tears. There is just something about watching your baby grow up that tugs on a mother's heart, especially when you're familiar with the teacher's history.

Justin's first-grade teacher had retired and now returned to teaching, and her knowledge and experience were a definite plus. Unfortunately, she had also acquired a reputation for speaking gruffly with the children, combined with matching facial expressions and body language. The hope and prayer was that she had mellowed in her later years. My mind reflects back to 1989, when Hurricane Hugo literally blasted the South Carolina coast. For many of us who were blessed to survive, the popular attire became t-shirts that proclaimed, "I Survived Hugo!" Well, our experience with first and second grade did not produce t-shirts, but we survived that experience! Actually, it wasn't as challenging as we thought it would be. Isn't it wonderful how the Lord hears and answers prayers? The results may not always be exactly what we had in mind, and it may not be what we want. However, Paul's counsel tells us in 1 Corinthians 1:25 (ERV) that even "*the foolishness of God is wiser than human wisdom.*"

Wisdom also tells us that change and challenges are inevitable as we matriculate through this life. One major change presented itself. Adjusting to a new environment can be challenging enough on its own for an adult (and even more so for a child), especially when it is combined with other complexities, such as your teacher being a family member — and not just any family member but Auntie Doris. Upon entering third grade, this could have gone one of two ways. It could have been a recipe for disaster or an opportunity for Justin to rise to the occasion and approach this situation in his own way. In private life, Doris Hanna-Jones was known as Auntie Doris; Justin's big brother, Donavan, who was previously her student, coined the title "Mountain Goat" to describe her in the classroom. Yikes!

Now, that was definitely a title difficult to ignore. It produced a laughable mental image of a teacher standing in the classroom with folded arms and a horn jutting from each side of her head. It also conjured up an image of leadership, power, and an unbending (or at least resistant) nature. Research on the mountain goat confirms the tendency of an unbending nature. Although this teacher was qualified, passionate and talented, the mountain goat portrayal was a fairly accurate description. Ironically, the dynamics of the goat family has similar applications to this classroom setting. As is with the goat family, in the classroom, there was a combination of nurturing and head-butting. Happily, though, the mountain goat imagery was more daunting than the actuality. This experience actually helped develop personal growth and expanded our capacity for flexibility.

Surprisingly, instead of diminishing ties between Auntie and nephew, it was sustained and enhanced. Interestingly, mild agitation is not always the enemy but a gateway to positive change and beauty. The transformation of a caterpillar to a butterfly is a prime example. The struggle is real, and yet without it, proper development can be lost.

Justin developed educationally, socially, physically, and spiritually. Unmistakably, this is the function of Christian education — to help with the development of the total person. Because our sons were avid readers, over the years we acquired enough books to create a public library. I feel that Justin's love and passion for a variety of reading genres and drawing helped broaden his outlook on life. He had a great sense of humor, good friends, and a deep love for his family. He loved his dad and their conversations about sports. As a sibling, there was, of course, sometimes sibling rivalry, but he had such admiration for his big brother. The things they shared in common knitted them together for life, while their differences broadened their capacity to accept people for who they are and where they are in life.

As for me, I have never been one to take parenting lightly. So, our relationship, even from the womb, was binding. As I turn back the pages in my mind, my heart is warmed remembering the sweet little ways that he expressed his love for me. There was a time when he was 5 years old, and he drew me an unrecognizable picture that was labeled, "To: Mommy, From: Justin." I am absolutely delighted as my mind reviews these pages of history. The sentiment of the drawing is more valuable than any Picasso or other famous artwork.

Being expressive through written and verbal communications and being athletic was all a part of his development process. Although, the spiritual development would become more and more apparent as positive changes and beauty continued to formulate, our desire for our children is for them to be well-rounded, which means fun must be a part of the process. Growing up, Justin particularly had fun playing basketball, and his competitive nature sometimes followed a testosterone-generated path of offensiveness. In this respect, he was truly his father's child.

During these formative years, there was lots of love; nevertheless, families are never free of challenges. Don and I worked hard to provide for our sons. Life was filled with worship, youth activities, family fun, and sibling rivalries. There were also some challenges that took the focus away from the care-free life a child is supposed to have. There were times when attention was directed toward other situations that pull on the strings of the heart, such as Don's emotional obstacles. During these times, I did what I could in an effort to make up for the oftentimes missing healthy emotional and physical presence of their father. For many years, Don was very active with multiple churches, organizations, and personal musical pursuits, in addition to his daytime job. Therefore, he spent a lot of time away from home; especially on the weekends. This made the need for family support even more critical.

Our sons were very close to both their maternal and paternal grandparents. My mother had been diagnosed with colon cancer. She had been in remission for a couple of years, but the cancer had now returned as a vengeful enemy. Grandma Essie, as she was known, passed away on February 13, 1999. Even though she was contending with the monstrosity of cancer, her death came suddenly and unexpectedly. The loss of this petite, quiet and yet strong-in-the-Lord, loving matriarch shook up our family's world like a violent tornado.

Donavan and Justin had both made Valentine's cards to give her the day that she passed away. Needless to say, my children were heartbroken, my father was devastated, and I had lost my mother and my dearest friend. Her death rocked our foundation. Donavan chose to attend the funeral, and at 5 years old, Justin knew that he did not want to see his dear grandmother like that. He chose not to attend the funeral, and we honored his request. Instead, he stayed with his Grandma Dot, who comforted him at home while we attended the services.

Although the days following were filled with uncertainty, pain, and loneliness, God brought us through this life storm. While Grandma Essie was certainly never forgotten, we embraced opportunities for love, laughter, and happiness, not only to help fill the void of life but also because these are characteristics of quality of life. One of those embracing moments came one day while we were at church in December of the same year. Justin simply and yet powerfully said, "I love you, Mommy." In a healthy environment, the bond between a mother and her children can be one of the strongest. In children, we can often see evidence of unconditional love. I could certainly see it in my sons. There's something quite special about the simplistic and innocent view of life that many children have.

> *"Unless you accept God's kingdom in the simplicity of a child, you'll never get in."* (Mark 10:13-16, MSG)

> *"Keep thy heart with all diligence; for out of it are the issues of life."* (Proverbs 4:23 KJV)

Chapter 4

Challenges That Do Not Cease to Amaze

*A*s I faced the challenges of grief and loss in my life that could not be ignored, it was time to make a decision about where Justin would attend high school. As parents, we want to make sure that we are making the right decisions for our children until they are at the point where they can make these choices for themselves. Even as parents, we are not wise enough to make these resolutions on our own. Don and I had many prayers and discussions about the various options for school. There were times when we were of the same mindset and other moments where we differed. Fortunately, we were able to come to an agreement in favor of Christian education, because it is such a beautiful thing when home, school, and church all blend together for the benefit of our children's educational, social, and spiritual needs.

His older brother attended Mount Pisgah Academy, but still, there was much to consider because each child is unique. After much time spent in prayer, the election was made that Justin would be attending Mount Pisgah Academy in Candler, North Carolina. The backdrop to the school is especially beautiful to me in the fall when the leaves are turning, and in the winter when the air is crisp and the mountains are snowcapped. Even though we would miss him dearly, God opened the door of opportunity in spite of our limited income. In addition, even though Justin loved his dad very much, it was an opportunity to find reprieve from the challenges of emotional and behavioral disorders in the home. Mental health is a real phenomenon; it's as real as physical health challenges. So, this Seventh-day Adventist Christian Academy would be the beginning of a new life adventure for us all.

July-December 2008

While attending the Christian boarding academy, Justin quickly made friends, and some would become lifelong companions. During Justin's time away, the climate in our home began to change. There was an unexpected life storm on the horizon. For years, Don had experienced emotional and behavior disorders, and now the effects of this condition seemed to intensify.

He was having more complaints about palpitations and thoughts of dying. He expressed with conviction that he did not want to kill himself but constantly felt as though he was dying. In desperation, he would sometimes pretend that he was suicidal because he knew that was the only way he would be admitted, and his case more thoroughly reviewed.

This feeling of dying combined with frequent palpitations increased the occurrence of frantic trips to various emergency rooms. In addition, there were complaints about feeling fatigued and briefly about some lower back discomfort. He was taking what could be described as a mountain of medications, and there are several that can cause fatigue; therefore, we felt sure this was the cause for the lethargy. Don repeatedly returned to the medical facilities and yet there seemed to be no improvement. As you can imagine, we were both overwhelmed and drowning in bewilderment.

One particular night after I was in bed, Don decided to drive himself to the Veteran's hospital, which was more than an hour away from where we lived. This time, after a more thorough examination, there was a suspicion of internal blood loss. In our wildest imaginations, the possibility of internal bleeding never entered our thoughts.

Now things were really becoming frightening, and I was not sure what was about to happen next. The lead doctor determined that a blood transfusion would be needed, and a diagnostic analysis did not immediately reveal the source of the blood loss. Additional testing would need to be done.

A few weeks later, we received notice that the culprit for the blood loss was potentially an enemy called multiple myeloma, which is typically a slow-moving cancer that forms in a type of white blood cell called plasma. Plasma cells help you fight infections by making antibodies that recognize and attack germs. Multiple myeloma causes cancer cells to accumulate in the bone marrow, where they crowd out healthy blood cells. Instead of producing antibodies that are helpful to the body, the cancer cells produce abnormal proteins that can wreak havoc on a person's body.

Needless to say, we were not prepared for what was about to come. A bone marrow biopsy was scheduled for September 15, 2008. A bone marrow biopsy can be a painful and risky procedure for some people. During this time, life was filled with an uncertainty that left an undeniably unsettling feeling within our hearts. We felt that it was important to keep our sons informed while trying not to alarm them until we knew more about the challenges that we were about to face. They had watched their father go in and out of the hospital on numerous occasions, but this time was very different. The mysterious source of blood loss was an anomaly that had not factored into our thoughts. It was certainly praying time. It was strengthening to know that family, friends, and spiritual leaders were praying along with us.

The day had come for the stressful but necessary bone marrow biopsy. Afterward, the physician reiterated that this is a slow-moving disease, and Don would likely be able to get some follow-up treatments locally. You can certainly imagine how relieved we all were to hear that news from the physician. Obviously, this was an emotional period in our lives, and emotions were heightened when just a few days later, Don was admitted into the hospital. Once again, his hemoglobin was low enough for yet another blood transfusion. The question that we are afraid to ask and yet dare not omit, and even demand at this point was, "Where is this blood coming from?!" The answer finally came that he was bleeding from the site of the biopsy. The blood had pooled into his left thigh, creating a huge and painful hematoma, and we soon learned that the initial diagnosis was wrong. While there are four stages in most cancer forms, there are only three with multiple myeloma, and unbelievably, Don was in advanced stage three.

From that point, his body was continuously deteriorating. I made arrangements for our sons to come see their father for what appeared would be their last time seeing him alive. Week after tormenting week, the body was visibly shutting down. There was increased blood pressure, excruciating pain, bleeding, kidney failure, extreme weakness, a reality of impending death, and then non-responsiveness. The bleeding seemed uncontainable. Even though the medical staff had been desperately and unsuccessfully working to stop the bleeding for hours, if there was not a drastic change, the impending end result would be unavoidable.

In the waiting room, family and friends were vigilant with me when the doctor called me out of the waiting room, and my pastor and brother, Daryl Anderson, came with me. The physician shared with me what I already knew in my heart and stated, "We tried to save him but could not stop the bleeding, and I am so sorry to say your husband has passed away."

Even though his death was impending, I still felt numb inside because it is impossible to totally prepare yourself to hear those life-changing words about your husband. Six harrowing weeks after entering the Veteran's hospital, Don took his last breath on October 31, 2008, at approximately 3 a.m.

For a few moments, it was like my ability to speak was gone. The past few weeks, in particular, I had intentionally suppressed emotions so that I could try to be coherent when speaking with family, friends, and doctors and when making decisions regarding Don's medical care. To be quite honest, my mind and body were so fatigued, I did not feel that I had the strength or energy needed to process my emotions as I watched Don's life slowly and painfully ebb away. Now, every emotion that I tried to suppress was cathartically released. I could not speak, but the tears flowed and flowed like a flooded river. Because the depth of my grief would not allow me to speak at that moment, my pastor and brother by choice went to the waiting room to speak with the family and friends that were there for support.

My heart was weary and heavy as I contemplated how I was going to tell our sons that their father had passed away. I needed to be the one to tell them, and it was my responsibility to be their anchor. I could not imagine them hearing it from someone else. We had just attended Grandma Belle's funeral in August, and I remember Justin saying that he did not want to have to attend any more funerals. First, my father had passed away six years prior, a critical male role model for my sons. Then, Granddaddy Jack passed away three years later, and that was hard; he was also a model for men and especially grandfathers. Now, I had to find a way to tell them about their father.

Unfortunately, I could not speak with Donavan in person since he lived in Alabama, but I called to share the heartbreaking news with him. Later, I notified the school and then took the two-and-a-half-hour drive so I could tell Justin in person and bring him home. I wanted to go alone because I needed the time to pray, process, and determine how I would tell him.

Donavan's pain was very apparent when I spoke with him, but he was able to talk about his emotions to some degree. Justin, on the other hand, vocally expressed very little. It was obvious that he was sad and hurting, but I could only tell what he was feeling inside through his body language, facial expressions, and vocal tones. There were no visible tears. Although grief is an individual process and everyone processes in their own way, I knew that he needed to be able to release those pent-up emotions. He kept his emotions bottled up inside until his aching heart could no longer contain itself, and finally, he broke down and cried and released much of his undeniable pain and mourning. I did my very best to console him and assure him of his father's love and how proud he was of him; he loved Donavan and Justin with all of his heart.

I remember feeling like I was in a fog as my mind turned toward preparing for the funeral. The days seemed surreal and endless as night after night, well-meaning family and friends came to visit. Their visits and prayers were very much appreciated, but I was so tired and just mentally and emotionally drained. I felt like I needed to be strong, especially for our sons. I wanted the service to be over as quickly as possible due to the sheer emotional and physical exhaustion.

Don was well known in the community as a gifted musician, and I remember the church being filled to capacity. I do not remember the eulogy, but I do remember the presentation of the flag. It is a representation of a person who honorably served their country. For me, it is also a representation of an organization that serves many veterans desperately needing assistance, and that not enough is being done to meet those needs.

"The last enemy to be destroyed is death."
(1 Corinthians 15:16, NLT).

After the service was completed, it was hard for my sons to get back into the routine of school. Understandably, the end of the school year was now filled with a myriad of thoughts and emotions that have nothing to do with core subjects and everything to do with human fragility. Life had taken on a new persona still so surreal and difficult to grasp. I was grateful that there was a good family support system for them, and it was a blessing that they both had Grandma Dot and Aunties to support them. They especially felt comfortable sharing their thoughts and emotions with Auntie Peaches. In addition, my heart rejoiced to know that Justin had good friends like Richard, and others for additional support. I thank God for our closely knitted relationship with my sons. It somehow made our loss a little bit easier to bear.

The rest of the semester was particularly challenging. After some time though, and over the remainder of his high school adventure, Justin threw himself into a variety of things that fit into one of two categories: "Amazing" or "Should Never Have Happened."

Amazing:
Loyal friend
Embraced multiple cultures
Passion for gymnastics
Love for history
Compassion for those less fortunate

Should Never Have Happened:
Skipped class
Participated in dorm pranks
Fell asleep in math class
Senior year suspension

Donavan appropriately described Justin's high school life when he said, "It was a checkered path." I would add "quite interesting."

"Because you know that the testing of your faith produces endurance." (James 1:3, NASB)

Chapter 5

Justin's High School Senior Year

*I*want to share with you what happened during my son Justin's senior year. As you know, the senior year is a very busy and exciting time. Oh, but my Justin! My baby had gotten suspended for an infraction at the beginning of his senior year. Needless to say, I was not a happy mom. I wasn't happy with Justin, nor was I happy with the administration. It felt like my thoughts, emotions, and word choices were as varied as a color spectrum. I went from disbelief to "Really? Really Justin? Are you kidding me?"

Even though we would be taking the long ride back home, his compassionate heart was still in full effect in spite of the circumstances. He pleaded with me to let him go by the manor nursing home to say goodbye to one of the residents that he promised to visit. I certainly could not look into those eyes and deny that honorable request. Later, I was sad because he was sad. I could tell that he was remorseful but would have to suffer the consequences of his choices. As you can imagine, the car ride home seemed to take twice as long as it took to arrive at the school. It allowed for a very long period of rumination.

It was not shared on the ride home, but in later discussions, I discovered that Justin still had a desire to complete his senior year at Mount Pisgah Academy. As it turned out, there were many of his friends and classmates who had the same desire. After much prayer, I enrolled him in a local high school, where he excelled socially and academically. He was an honor roll student and a member of an organization called "Men of Distinction." I had an opportunity to speak with his teachers, and they all had such positive things to say. They used words such as: "Intelligent," "well-mannered," "funny" and one in particular commented on how much she enjoyed his gymnastics skills.

Because of his love and passion for gymnastics, I found a gym where he could practice and be a member of a local team. Although my desire for my children to receive a Christian education had never changed, with graduation just five months away, I could be described as reluctantly content. In my mind, at this stage in Justin's educational journey, he would be graduating high school from my old alma mater, Wilson High School, home of the purple and gold Tigers.

In spite of the circumstances that lead Justin to be home at this time, I enjoyed our time together. Particularly enjoyable were the times that we spent in worship together and the times that we spent in laughter. Justin was somewhere between being a baby and trying to find his way into manhood. He also enjoyed our time at home. He would often put his head on my shoulder and always gave me great big bear hugs. However, there was still something missing because he still desired to graduate with his class at Mount Pisgah Academy.

The return to Christian education was still on Justin's agenda for his senior year. His good friend, Richard, was acting as his attorney, gathering information and pleading his case to sympathetic ears. He would then consult with his determined and eager client. Justin decided he would write a letter to the appropriate council at the academy. He shared his plan with me, and my response was simple: "If you feel that is the way that God is leading you, then move forward." To be quite honest, it was almost the end of the first semester at Mount Pisgah Academy, and I did not have much faith in the plan.

Justin was holding himself accountable, and I had to stand by his side even though my faith in the plan was somewhere between minimal and zero. The plan was set into motion with the submission of the letter. The letter stated...

Dear Staff,
I like to start off this letter by saying believe it or not I really do miss all of you. I know this might sound cliché, but you really don't know what you have until it is taken away from you. I have had ample time to think about what I have done, and I am so sorry. I have disappointed you as staff, the student body, my mother, and most importantly God. I honestly feel that Pisgah is the best place for me to grow spiritually and educationally. You might ask yourself what is different from the last time, so I'll tell you. I understand now the importance of a good Christian education where we as a body can do His work and we all are on one accord. Pisgah is a good influence on me and the friends you make here you keep for a lifetime. Believe me when I say my whole mindset has changed. I want to make better choices and I always want to do the right thing always, with God's help. I am more than positive that Pisgah will help enhance my spiritual walk with Him.

Finally, there was a response from the school. Justin would be returning to the academy his second semester of his senior year! You can imagine what Justin was feeling. He was ecstatic! He was keenly aware that God hears and answers prayers of repentant teenagers too. We must always remember that, in every situation, it is not man but God that has the final say. (Proverbs 16:1)

At that moment, God had opened up the Red Sea and had given the sign to move forward, and like the children of Israel, we moved in faith. Once again, we made the trip to Asheville, North Carolina. This time, the atmosphere was different, and Justin was determined to succeed with more intensity and focus than ever before. If there was going to be a movie written about the second half of my son's senior year, it would be simply titled, *The Return of Justin Emanuel Hanna: Purposed and Driven*.

He was self-assured, mischievous, suave, humorous, and my baby. Justin was a young man trying to find his way in life while dealing with the recent loss of his father and others that were close to him. This young man felt called to be back to this place in the mountains and determined to continue a path of success throughout the duration of his senior year and beyond. As a parent, I had to trust God and the positive traits and encouragement that I poured into my children. I did not have faith in the plan, but I had faith in my child, and I praise God for working with us through this situation.

This path of success was quite obvious. The semester was almost perfect from the onset for several reasons. Justin witnessed God's favorable answer to his prayer. He returned in January with a 3.3 GPA, he and his best friend Richard entered the annual talent show and won in their category, and he rejoined the gymnastics team as a dedicated courageous team member. I later learned that the only way the coach would allow him to rejoin the team was if the team voted him back in. The favorable vote was unanimous, and at the end of the school year, Justin received a gymnastics award for his accomplishments.

Finally, the climactic moment of the year had arrived. It was time to take the march across the stage as a 2011 graduate. Justin was about to see the full unveiling of answered prayer. Donavan and I watched with bated breath as he marched across the stage. It was a proud, joyful, and solemn moment. Our family was there in full support. There was Grandma Dot, Auntie Peaches, Auntie Nette, Auntie Margaret, Uncle Douglas, and Auntie Lola, as well as his loving, supportive cousins. Auntie Doris and Uncle Walter had driven all night to be there. It was a blessed and grand occasion. A determined young man walked away knowing that God answers prayer. Justin moved forward feeling victorious, confident, and looking forward to the future.

"When we invite Him, Jesus will take up residence in the middle of every situation, especially one that involves your child's spiritual development."
Vanessa Hanna-Verrett

Chapter 6

Precious Moments

*I*f there is anything that seemingly produces a time warp, it's anticipation. When will we hear from the university? Why is it taking so long? What will the response be? Finally, the day came when the acceptance letter arrived! We would be headed to Oakwood University!

We were excited about the news and yet had mixed emotions. Many of us know from experience, and others can imagine, how much preparation goes into sending your child to college. The preparation is magnified when the school is approximately 500 miles away. I remember being more concerned about how to get Justin and all of his belongings to Oakwood than the eight-hour drive it would take to get there.

The thoughts were jumping around in my mind like popcorn in an air popper. Should I rent a small truck? The largest truck I've ever driven is a small, two-seater, 1996 Mazda B2300 pick-up truck. My truck is much smaller than a U-Haul truck, and the thought of driving it across three states for eight hours or more was a little daunting.

My brain continued to look for other options. I wondered if I should rent a trailer. It was not as big as a truck, I reasoned, but neither have I towed a trailer before. Neurons were firing like crazy all over my brain as I tried to recall a vague memory about how to back up a trailer. I once heard that attempting to back up a trailer can be very challenging for the inexperienced. Oh my! As a single parent, you can imagine all of the question marks in my mind. I didn't know the answers to my questions, but I was keenly aware that God is able, and somehow, He will work it out.

Moving day had come! It was a sunny day, and we were ready for travel with a trailer in tow. It will be yet another adventurous chapter in our lives. Although the future is uncharted and exciting, this was also a time of contemplation because a lot has happened over the last few years. This contemplation gave way to sadness and disappointment.

I recall we had been driving for an hour when something unusual and disturbing happened. Across from me, on the passenger side, quiet, sobbing sounds were heard. Naturally, I was alarmed. The day was beautiful, and the drive was great. "What is wrong, baby?" Somehow, I was not ready physically or emotionally for his response. With intense emotion, he said, "I wish my dad were here to see me going to college." My heart melted like butter in a sizzling hot pan, and although there was not a cloud in the sky, my tears flowed in an unexpected torrential downpour along with his, which forced me to pull over on the side of the road, since my salty tears made my eyes sting and added difficulty to clearly see the road.

Once safely off of the road, I gave my baby boy one of the biggest hugs that I could muster and shared with him how much his dad loved him and how very proud he would have been. Then, after a round of tissue and bathroom breaks, we were back on the road to continue our anticipated journey. We knew where we were going, but the future lay ahead, waiting to be discovered.

Finally, the eight hours passed, and we arrived. Richard and Justin had been talking continuously along the way as we traveled. The "bros," as they called each other, were really anticipating this university adventure. We drove up to the school, and the parking area was filled with vehicles, which further complicated my situation of having to tow this unfamiliar, awkward trailer. To make things even worse, I was now in a situation that required me to back up. *Ugh! Really? Oh my!*

Up to this point, I had been able to avoid the infamous back-up procedure, but it looked like I was about to face that fear head-on. It was pretty challenging for me to try to coordinate the movement of my vehicle with the movement of the trailer. As you can imagine, what was happening with me was not a pretty sight.

Fortunately, a gentleman who saw and felt my pain came to my rescue. Even though he was a stranger, I was grateful and gladly turned the wheel over to him. Thankfully, the car was turned around successfully, and we excitedly headed to the building where registration was taking place. Excitement was soon combined with moans as we looked at the sea of people in the various lines. Nevertheless, we had come this far... through death, through tears, through hundreds of miles on the road, those lines would not deter us. Finally, registration was complete, and soon afterward, Justin was settled into the dorm. None of it could have been accomplished without God's grace and mercy, and I am ever so thankful.

"We've come this far by faith and depending on Jesus."

Even though Justin attended Academy during high school, college was an adjustment, but he was doing it by God's grace. It seemed like we had just gotten registered, and suddenly it was time for Thanksgiving break. The family decided Thanksgiving dinner this year would be held in Nashville, Tennessee, and there was a large gathering of family members and friends who began to pour into the Music City from South Carolina, North Carolina, Georgia, and Alabama.

Donavan drove up from Alabama with his brother and Justin's good friend, Richard. Dinner, of course, was late, but we had a wonderful time that year. There was a lot of laughter and tears as we remembered those who were no longer with us and lots of delectable dishes. We relished our time together through the weekend. Then, it was time to take the journey back through the various pathways to our everyday lives and responsibilities. For Justin, this meant getting back to focusing on ending the semester on a positive note.

"There are few things more special than family."

Christmas Time

There was less than a month left before the end of the first semester and *wow*, the tall order of successfully completing the first semester of college was done! Justin was ready to come home and just do nothing for a few days. I was happy he was finding his way in the world, and at the same time, I was ready for him to come home too. This Christmas, it would just be Justin and I. It would have been nice to have had them both at home for the holiday, but Donavan was working and unable to travel home because of his schedule. I was trying to figure out the details. What will we have for dinner? Will we invite anyone else over? What about decorations?

Although it was decided it would just be the two of us, I was surprisingly inspired to bake a turkey. I am a vegetarian, but my son did not consider himself to be a vegetarian, which basically meant that, like his dad, he ate both vegetarian dishes and meat dishes. Nevertheless, I was inspired to bake him a turkey.

What I want you to understand is that this is a decision of mammoth proportion for me. Since I became a vegetarian more than 20 years ago, I do not enjoy even touching uncooked meats. Of course, I have cooked chicken and beef prior to becoming a vegetarian, and since then on a few occasions. However, my late husband primarily prepared all of the meat dishes. Therefore, it had been years since I had cooked meat of any kind, and I was truly outside of my comfort zone because I had never cooked a whole turkey in my entire life. Amazingly, I was about to attempt to cook that bird. I laugh as I think about how my son's taste buds were about to be either very fortunate or very unfortunate. Nevertheless, I was undaunted by these facts and was mentally as well as physically ready to tackle this challenge.

I began my process by consulting with others who were known to be turkey-cooking experts, as well as the internet. Next, I began to look for just the right turkey. Some may wonder how a turkey-cooking novice would determine if it was the right turkey. Well, it needed to be small-to-medium and drug-free. Happily, I found the perfect turkey along with my other ingredients. After preparing the turkey, I popped it into the oven and when it was time to serve our meal, I watched my son with intent eyes as I looked for some kind of reaction. When he tasted it and kept eating, I could then give a sigh of relief. After all of that effort, you can imagine how happy I was. Yes! My mission had been successfully accomplished!

My next favorite time of the year is Christmas, and my next "precious moments" story is one of my favorites.

The Christmas Gift

My joy continued when Justin presented me with my Christmas gift. I remember he had received some funds from a family member. One thing Justin wanted to do with the money was buy me some perfume. Of course, it could not be just any perfume. It had to be *Chance* by Chanel. As I think back on this event, I am curious about how he selected *Chance* as the ideal perfume for me. I can imagine that the person at the perfume counter made some suggestions, and he smelled various fragrances until he found the one he believed to be the right one for his mom.

He had never selected perfume for me before, so this was something quite special. However, when he told me what he planned to do, I tried to discourage him because the perfume was going to cost about $100! I did not want him to spend that much of his money on a gift for me. Well, I may as well had been talking to the wind because Justin was determined to get that perfume for me. Reluctantly, I gave in to his persistence. Quite honestly, I was actually experiencing multiple emotions regarding this gift. There was financial concern, joy, and of course, love. My heart was overflowing with joy because I knew that presenting me with this perfume was one of his ways of showing how much he loved, respected, and valued me as his mother.

When I received the perfume from my son, it came with some special instructions that he shared with me. It was almost hysterical to me because he was so serious when he was relaying the instructions. I remember those instructions as if it were yesterday. He said, "Mom, you only need three squirts." I do not know if that is what the lady at the counter told him or if it was because he knew if I used it up quickly, he would not have the funds to replace it. Those words reverberate in my mind. "Mom, you only need three squirts." My senses have never been exposed to a more wonderful fragrance. The value of the perfume is priceless. Children are a gift from God.

"No matter how old they get, they are still our children and the quality-time shared is invaluable."

Chapter 7

It Is A New Year...Now What?

I am sure that many of you remember what it was like being on a holiday break from school. For a lot of people, it always seemed as if the break period moved forward at high speed, and before you know it, the time to go back had come. The holidays were behind, and it was time for Justin to get back to the grind of focusing on school again, exercising, and envisioning what the future looks like.

He found the first semester to be challenging, but he was not about to throw in the towel. One of his and Donavan's favorite movies has a scene where someone longingly talks about the things that they could have done — unfulfilled opportunities. However, in Justin's personal life, he did not want "unfulfilled" to play an intricate role in his life effort. Justin found himself becoming more aware of himself both intellectually and spiritually as he took time out for introspective surveys.

The results of this personal rumination surfaced in various ways over the next three months. My son, his good friend Richard, and his new friend Ephraim were being more conscientious regarding sharpening study tactics. The goal was to just be more intentional... more focused regarding life choices. In addition, it was unknown to me until months later that in January, Justin had a conversation with a friend of his from high school, Joseph Luis. They enjoyed sharing what each had been experiencing since graduation in May 2011. During the conversation, Justin raised a profound point that flesh and blood did not reveal to him. What Justin said to his friend is "Only what you do for Christ will last." To me, this was a mark of spiritual growth that every Christian parent wants to see reflected in their child (or children). My heart overflowed with joy when I heard about this conversation... "Only what you do for Christ will last." Wow!

This mature, penetrating, and philosophical statement had a lasting impact on his friend's life, and perhaps more than Justin could imagine at the time. What was even more powerfully impacting about this one though, was the fact that it was not something that was spoken with the intention of impressing his friend because that was not his personality. When Justin spoke, he spoke from the heart, and it could be something that you wanted to hear or something you wished you had discouraged. Either way, it would be an honest assessment of how he felt about a situation. So that comment could be considered the glowing phrase of the month for January.

The month of February is most often associated with the emotion of love predominantly because of Valentine's day. How do I know this? Well, I have lived on this earth for a number of years and have learned a few things. In addition, according to *USA Today*, in 2016, there were $19.7 billion spent on Valentine's Day gifts and/or celebrations in the United States alone! Wow, that is a ginormous amount of love expressions.

There are so many different ways to show love outside of making purchases, and please hear me when I say this: I am not opposed to receiving gifts. I love it! One of the best gifts that I have ever been given came to me as a surprise during this month when billions of dollars are spent to express this emotion. What could that gift possibly have been you may wonder? How much did it cost? Where did it come from? Those are all great questions.

Though it held little monetary value, it was worth more than gold to hear my baby ask me these cherished words and sentiments: "Mom, can we start praying together?"

As shocked as I was, my response was "Yes!" and I quickly added, "Can we also share a devotional though?"

His response of "Yes" was like the melodious sound of a harp being channeled through my heart.

There was much rejoicing on earth and in heaven over this request! It revealed Justin Emanuel Hanna in the process of becoming. Becoming is a profound place to be in a person's life, and I absolutely love how Aristotle defined it as "… a movement from the lower level of potentiality to the higher level of actuality." We began the process of incorporating prayer and devotional thought on a regular basis. However, this was not the end of the metamorphosis of a teenager to a young man.

I knew that he had set his sights on functioning within the legal system. Additional confirmation came when he called me to share his desire to work as an intern in a congressional office in the summer of 2012. So, I told him that I knew someone that I would contact. Although this was on my list of things to do, my intent was to make the call soon, but not necessarily immediately. However, that young man would not let me rest until I had accomplished my task. It seemed his next focal point was hinged on the achievement of my assignment — and failure was not an option. He was really intent and excited regarding the possibility of this internship taking place. Finally, the connection was made and a plan in place for his summer escapade in a congressional office. I was happy that it was all working out to his satisfaction.

It was now the end of February, with March rapidly approaching. My son, Donavan, had a small surgical procedure at the end of February, and thankfully, the procedure was successful. I decided to drive to Huntsville at this time since it would allow me to see both of my sons. In addition, this visit would coincide with the beginning of spring break, and Justin would be coming home with me. In my mind, it would be somewhat of a road trip for us, and this thought made me laugh because he and Donavan had previously stated that the two of them would go on a road trip. However, I would not be permitted to go because, for some odd reason, they thought I would somehow spoil their fun. I wonder where they got that idea from?

Unlike the drive to Huntsville at the beginning of the school year, this drive to Huntsville was fortunately uneventful as I arrived during the middle of the week. However, as the weekend approached, also escalating was the threat of a tornado looming on the horizon. That potential menace darkened my plans of leaving to head back home on Friday, March 3, 2012, and there was also a delay in students being released from the university because of the threatening weather. This city is known as a "tornado alley." What was even more dubiously impressive is its high ranking in the nation for top tornado cities. I prayed that these extremities would be subdued, and thankfully, they were, but by the time this climatic weather had subsided, it was too late to begin our journey home and we would have to leave the next morning instead. We settled in with food and worship at Donavan and Ariel's apartment as the beginning of the Sabbath approached on that Friday evening. The three of them were more like siblings than cousins which made that time even more special.

Sabbath morning was a major contrast to the gloom of Friday. It was a beautiful, blue-skied, sunny day. We packed up the car, hugged and kissed Donavan goodbye, and started our road trip home. Justin slept most of the way between Huntsville and Atlanta, and as we were approaching Atlanta, I was getting a little sleepy and my stomach began giving me signs that it was time to eat again. Although we had food in the car, my thoughts are that a home-cooked meal would be even better. So, I called my sister-in-law, Margaret, to see if they were home from church yet. She estimated that they would likely be there by the time we arrived at their home. That was good news to me, but Justin was quite reluctant to stop. He was anxious to get home and just wanted to keep driving. So, as a natural negotiator, I said to him, "Let us go there as discussed, and if for some reason, they were not at the house yet, we would wait for a few minutes and then get back on the road." Our family did not arrive after a short wait. So, after a quick phone call, to Justin's delight, we were soon back on the road.

Driving down Interstate 20 was getting us closer to home, and conveniently, we had food in the car to take care of the hunger. However, the fact that I was still sleepy was unresolved. Justin had his permit, but his driving skills had not been interstate-tested yet, and I wasn't quite ready to test them on this particular trip. The next rest stop would be our destination. Have you ever been so tired while driving that the rest stop seemed like it was hundreds of miles away when actually it was only just a few miles in the distance? I started to feel just like that.

What helped to make me feel less tired was laughing at a comment that Justin made when I said, if we had waited longer in Atlanta, I may not have been as sleepy now. He said "No! No! We need to get home." The wording in itself was not funny, but when combined with the emphatic manner in which it was said, it was quite funny! It reminded me of my niece who also has a sense of humor and emphatic tendencies at times. I don't know if I was tired to the point of delirium or what, but I laughed so much that I decided to call my niece, Anita, who lived in Las Vegas, Nevada.

As I was making the call, I was uncertain if I would reach her at that particular time of the day. Happily, she answered, allowing me to share that her cousin had somehow begun using one of her familiar phrases. After telling her about it, she quickly took off with it, saying "No! No, he doesn't have to stop at auntie's house today if he doesn't want to." The three of us just laughed and laughed. Looking back, perhaps we were all delirious.

Just when it seemed an exit would never appear, the road sign showed we were almost there; we arrived at the exit for a much-needed break. After taking a break and refreshing ourselves, we were about to get back on the road when someone startled me by tapping on my window. Typically, I travel alone, and I do not wind down my window to speak with strangers. In the meantime, Justin is expressing, "Ma, they might need some help."

Cautiously, I rolled down the window a portion of the way and listened to the stranger's plight. They were traveling, and their car broke down. Justin's heart was touched as he urged me to give them a contribution. I was somewhat fixated on whether this was a true story or not. Nevertheless, I submitted to the request and gave the man a contribution for him and his family. As we drove away and before merging into traffic, Justin said, "Ma, we could have given them more money."

I'm thinking, "That's really easy for you to say when it's not your money," but I did not voice that thought. Instead, I asked, "How do you know they were telling the truth?"

His quick but thought-provoking response was, "How do you know they were not?"

That was an excellent question coming from a compassionate heart, and it made me really think about how we should be willing to help those who are less fortunate without judgement or reservation as guided by the Holy Spirit.

The rest of the eight-hour trip was filled with conversation, laughter, and sleep for Justin. I was reflecting as I drove, and I was happy that Justin would be home for spring break. His question continued to resonate with me. His 18 years of life had served him well, and in a world filled with hate, my son was compassionate regarding the misfortune of others.

"Be kind to one another, tender-hearted, forgiving one another..."
(Ephesians 4:32, ESV)

Chapter 8

The March Winds

*M*arch is considered the first month of spring, which is a season that is associated with new beginnings as life sprouts new leaves; it's also an ending to winter, the change of a season. In addition, it is also known for tempestuous weather, and I am so grateful that none of that showed up while driving home. However, what did show up is Justin's enthusiasm about officially beginning his vacation now that we had arrived home.

Even though I had to work during the week, I made sure that I carved out time for us to spend time hanging out. Justin spent lots of time, especially during the day, talking with his friends. Even though he and his high school friends had gone their separate ways after graduation, he maintained close connections with many of them. So along with Richard, Ephraim, Donavan, and Monique, he also spent a lot of time talking with his friend Lillian, and others whose names I cannot even begin to recall.

One evening, while Justin and I were out for dinner, he was doing a lot of multitasking. While speaking with me, he was also constantly texting. Imagine that in a millennial world. I remember telling him that I needed him to focus on our conversation, and his comment was, "But Ma, I'm talking to both of you." He explained that his friend was in crisis mode, and apparently, he was coaching regarding the situation. However, my son, the counselor, assured me that he was almost done.

I suggested that he consider counseling as a career choice since people trusted his advice, and because he seemed to function in that capacity quite often. With a half-smile, and an air of self-assurance, he responded that counselors did not make enough money, so he would stick to the legal profession. We broke out into laughter which continued throughout the week.

Other things that we enjoyed during the week included "bring your son to work day," which is one that Justin and I created. He spent half the day with me at work and decided that he did not like my job or any job that required him to be in the same office all day. However, that did not stop him from relaxing in my office before we left for lunch. As the week continued, we spent time at the gym because Justin loved being physically fit and so did I. As a self-proclaimed fitness coach, he also enjoyed encouraging and coaching others to become more physically fit. He worked with several of his friends such as Chelsey and Joseph Luis before even leaving for college. They were well pleased to have him as their personal coach. Justin gave me several exercise assignments too, and although I embrace being healthy, at that time, I was not quite as enthusiastic about the grind as my son was.

One of the more fun days for me though was when he and I went shopping. Have you ever noticed how our children excel with spending their parents' money? Justin bought a pair of red TOMs shoes, which provided casual but stylish comfort. More than that, he loved the fact that for every pair of shoes purchased, the company provides a pair for a needy child. This was another way that he illustrated his desire to help the disadvantaged, and since I paid for the shoes, I was contributing to the cause as well.

My personal shopping was not tied to a noble cause such as the one that Justin supported; I just needed to pick up a few things. I remember us walking down a strip mall when a particular store caught my interest. We went into the store and began looking around. Justin's style was unique and suave, and he wanted no less for me. He was very attentive in helping me select a pair of sunglasses. I then meandered over to the dress department where there were various colors and styles. Occasionally, I would say, "What do you think about this dress, Justin?" He always responded with an honest opinion and finally, we discovered one that we thought would work well for me. A revelation far more charming than the dress was discovered on this shopping spree.

As we continued talking, it was shared that my son had an ulterior motive for assisting me. Something that weighed heavily on his heart and mind was that he did not want me to be alone. He wanted me to be prepared to meet the person who was meant for me. Wow! My heart was overflowing to know that my 18-year-old son was so concerned, not just about my physical well-being, but also about my social and emotional well-being. At that moment, I could have easily bought him another pair of shoes. Now Donavan was not quite there yet, and his mentality was in the realm of "who do I need to put in a headlock for trying to date my mother?" Ha! He is also good at making me laugh! I would not trade these guys for anyone else and could not love either one of them more.

Have you ever noticed how swiftly time seems to pass when you are having a really good time? The week seemed to have come to an end so quickly, and it was time to get ready for worship at our church on Sabbath morning. I settled into my seat with one of my friends, and I looked around for Justin, who was sitting by himself on the opposite side of the church looking as if in deep thought. I made eye contact to invite him to come over to sit with me. He accepted the invitation and promptly came over and put his head on my shoulder. Yes, you could say that he took his status as a baby quite seriously, and he was not concerned about who witnessed this act of affection and neither did I. These were extra special moments since he would be taking the train that night to head back to school. In addition, there was also an air of excitement since this would be Justin's first train ride.

We needed to be at the train station by 10 p.m., and it was a two-hour drive to the station. So, I arranged for a friend to go along with us and that would alleviate me driving back alone at night. Once we arrived in Charlotte, we stopped to get something to eat, and then on to the train station. While waiting for boarding time, Justin stretched his long, six-foot body across the wooden bench and laid his head in my lap. Again, there was no concern regarding a baby-ish image. He was very comfortable and confident in who he was, and at that moment, he was with his mom, and that was all that mattered. Boarding time came, along with prayers for travel safety for him and Donavan (because his big brother would be traveling to meet him at the train station).

Unexpectedly, the train's arrival in Birmingham, Alabama was delayed due to a gruesome accident. It seemed there was what appeared to be a homeless man that was lying on the tracks in the path of the oncoming train and unfortunately, the massive iron structure could not stop in time to avoid colliding with the frail body that laid in its path. There are two main thoughts that weighed on my mind. First, my heart was saddened by this tragedy. Secondly, what an experience for a first train ride. Thankfully, the duration of the trip passed by without further incident, and Justin arrived safely and in the car with his brother. As you can imagine, he somehow had to put the terrible tragedy in the background and reflect on the task ahead ... successfully finishing up the second semester of his first year of college.

"... soaring on wings like eagles." (Isaiah, 40:31)

Chapter 9

The Raging Storm...
Unanticipated...Unprepared...

Whatever the task ahead, it should always encompass the question, "What must I do on this life journey to get one step closer to Christ?" Justin was seeking a deeper relationship with the God of the universe. One week after he returned from spring break, he and Ephriam attended an event that was being held at Southern Adventist University that weekend, and it was surprising to Justin how much that service impacted him.

He and Ephriam arrived late for the service and had to sit in the very front of the auditorium. Initially, they weren't thrilled about the seating arrangement, but consequently, they were both quite pleased about it since it afforded them a close encounter with the speaker whose message was intense and spiritually impacting. He described it as the best service he had ever attended, and my heart swelled with thanks and praises to God for the work He was doing in Justin's life through the Holy Spirit.

This trend continued into the next week, which was the week of March 23, 2012, and was filled with uncommon events. At the beginning of the week, Justin reached out to his friend, Ellie, because he knew that she would be having knee surgery and wanted her to know that he was thinking about her and praying for a successful surgery. Because their conversations were typically filled with laughter and jokes, she was a little surprised by the sincerity she heard in his tone. There was a recognition that she was seeing a more serious side of Justin.

That was not the only anomaly that took place during the week. I have a niece who was having some challenges with her teenage son, and she called me out of the blue because she wanted Justin to speak with him. When I spoke with Justin about this request on Wednesday, March 21, his initial response was light and jovial, "What? Am I a counselor?"

I laughed and said, "Justin, just call him." He agreed to call him and carried out that promise.

Continuing on with that week, here was the jaw-dropper for me: Justin shut down his Facebook page. I was really surprised when he told me about that, and being a mom who is naturally curious, I asked, "Why?"

He responded to me with the same seriousness that I am sure Ellie witnessed. In fact, he sounded very mature and resolute as he explained, "I shut down my Facebook page because I just want to be focused." As a mom, I was so proud of him for having made that decision. Hearing those words caused my heart to swell.

It was now Friday, March 23. Relaxation from the week was almost here and I was certainly looking forward to winding down from the week. Justin did not have a heavy school schedule on Friday which afforded him and his brother an opportunity to have lunch together on campus that day. Later that same day, I received a call that ended in a request for money after a brief conversation.

Now, what parent has not received that call? Well, I had just given him money for something that he wanted to purchase, and I gently gave him a crash course on economics. As I recall though, it was not a definite "no," but I wanted him to think about it, and he was thoughtful. Justin did not get upset, nor did he try to persuade me. He listened to me, and we continued to talk for a few moments longer before the conversation ended with "I love you, Justin."

He responded with, "I love you too, Mommy." It struck my attention briefly because he typically only used 'mommy' when he was playing or really setting into his role as the baby. However, neither one of those descriptions seemed to apply in this conversation.

I clearly remember it was a sunny day and unseasonably warm, but a few hours later, when the next phone call came from Donavan, a sunny day suddenly turned cloudy. Thoughts of relaxation gave way to concern.

Donavan's voice was calm but tense and with a slight but noticeable hesitation. He told me Justin had been in an accident. It seemed that he was trying to process what he wanted to say, and I was suddenly panicked while straining to remain as calm as possible.

What happened? Was he OK? I remember him saying that he was swimming and hit his head. Oh, my God! Then he told me that he was in the ambulance headed to the hospital. He promised to call back as soon as he got more information.

I briefly spoke with my supervisor, and then as swift as the gulf stream current, I was out of the building while praying the entire time ... "Oh God! Please let him be OK!"

While driving home, I called my mother-in-law to tell her to pray and to call the prayer group so they could pray too. I also called my sister-in-law, Jackie, because she was in Nashville, Tennessee, and could get to him quicker than I could. She immediately agreed to go to Huntsville.

Now that I was at home and people were praying, my mind raced, always returning to one desperate thought: "I've got to get out of here and get to my baby."

My pastor was calling different airlines and getting others to help search for the quickest flight to Huntsville. Then, of all times, there were no flights leaving Florence or leaving from a nearby city at a time that would allow me to drive there and make the flight. In the meantime, I was throwing some items in a suitcase which included the devotional book that Justin and I would read from when we spoke and prayed over the phone.

Finally, it was decided that my pastor's wife would drive me to Atlanta and from there, my in-laws would drive me the rest of the way to Huntsville. The same thought was still with me: "I've got to get there! I've got to see my baby, and I want him to know that I'm there!"

Additionally, I needed to talk to the doctors and make sure that they did everything possible! My suitcases were in the car, and I was turning the lock on the door when a voice behind me said, "Don't lock the door. Let's go back inside. The voice was trying to stop my progress, but I could not be stopped.

With firm authority, I said "No, I've got to go. I've got to get to my baby. I've got to get to Justin."

The voice persists... It's my pastor. "Let's go inside." In my heart, in the depths of my soul, I knew what he was going to say, but it simply could not be. My heart could not comprehend, did not want to believe what my ears were hearing in his yet unspoken words.

There was a battle going on between my flesh and a reality that I did not want to accept. I was overwhelmed, and from somewhere deep inside of me came a bellowing scream,

NO! My heart was broken... torn into millions of tiny pieces like shattered glass, and I was certain it could not ever be put back together again. I was left with a gaping wound bleeding profusely, and there was no clotting factor in sight, nor consolation.

My pastor made an effort to console me, but I was inconsolable... He tried to finish the statement, but I wouldn't let him. I was walking around and around the room, muttering out loud, yet to myself... "This can't be! Oh, my God... Can this really be?"

It is unequivocally a parent's nightmare! Everything around me is dark. Isaiah 60:2 took on a new meaning, "*See, darkness covers the earth and thick darkness is over the peoples.*"

It was March 23, 2012, just three years and five months since my late husband's death. It couldn't be true... and then another rush of stabbing, piercing pain reached the core of my heart. My pastor still wanted to console me, but I wouldn't let him because to receive consolation would mean that it was true! *But it couldn't be true!*

I was still walking around, and around, and around the room, and I couldn't stop, because stopping would mean facing a horrid reality that I was not prepared for or willing to face.

"Oh, my God, this cannot be true! What do I do now? How can I survive this raging storm?"

Somehow, I still needed to get to Huntsville, because I must see him for myself. Chelsey, a personal friend of Justin's and a friend of our family, volunteered to drive me to Atlanta, and from there, my brother and sister-in-law would take me the rest of the way to Huntsville, Alabama. Although it was difficult to realize the full impact of the support at that time because of the numbing effect of my pain, there was a lot of love and support in that car on that dark night coming from Chelsey, Salisha, and Deloris.

We drove and drove until the sudden jolting movement of the car broke the silence. A tire blew out and the rim came off. Shortly after that, things got a little better because, surprisingly, Douglas and Margaret had arrived. Instead of waiting for us to get to Atlanta, they began driving toward us. I don't know how they got there so quickly, but they did, and just as quickly, my things were transferred into their car and we drove straight to Huntsville.

Although I have driven to Huntsville on numerous occasions over the years, never did the journey seem so long as it did on that dark, devastating, dreadful night. It seemed ten times longer than the actual eight hours, but we finally arrived. Ahead of our arrival, the university had made hotel arrangements. I went to the hotel until I could get to the funeral home to view his body, and Donavan, who was a great comfort to me. He joined me at the hotel and was with me the entire time.

We arrived at the funeral home, and even though I was now looking at his still, lifeless body, my heart still did not want to believe, and so it continued to break. I really did not think it could break any further, but I was so wrong. He looked very peaceful, as if he was just sleeping. From the depths of my soul, I wanted him to *please* wake up, get up and give me one of his special bear hugs. I never dreamed that I would kiss the lifeless body of my son, but I did that day, because it was not just a corpse; it was my baby lying there. I have had many heart-wrenching losses... my oldest brother, my mother, my father, my late husband, but none of them prepared me for the loss of my child. If you are a parent who has lost a child, you will know exactly what I mean. The ominous storm continues to rage.

The school planned a candlelight vigil, which my Donavan and I attended, along with my in-laws who brought me to Huntsville. It was a blur, but I remember a few things, such as a host of Oakwood students who formed a line that seemed to go on for miles. They each shared how Justin had touched their lives in one way or another.

One said, "I didn't really know him, but when we would see each other, he always spoke to me in such a way that made me feel like I was important."

Others said, "He was in my class and was always nice."

Others admired his gymnastic abilities.

To his friends, he was a brother and a leader.

I wished that I had a recording so that I could listen over and over and over again to what each one had to say. That night, my pillow was constantly wet with tears. The trip from Huntsville would be dramatically different this time.

Back at home, we had to plan and prepare for the friends and family who would be coming to our home to share condolences. I was very thankful for the support of Donavan, who was also deeply grieving. In addition, the support of family and friends was priceless. My niece from Las Vegas jumped on a plane without any luggage, just a few items in her purse, and arrived as quickly as she possibly could.

Although there was a foreboding tug of war between reality and desire which left me in a fog of sorts, a funeral service still had to be planned. If I can just be honest with you, it required more strength than I ever thought could be mustered. I could never have done it in my own strength.

I was very grateful for all of the support and love shown from the staff and students of Mount Pisgah Academy. Before the service began, each student walked up and placed a rose in a beautiful vase, and each long-stemmed rose had a beautiful little tribute note attached to it. My heart was touched by the gymnastics team, who came in uniform. Justin had such a passion for gymnastics, and he felt honored to have been a part of the team.

There are some parts of the service that remain unclear in my mind, but what was clear was that the service was beautiful. Donavan sang a beautiful and emotional medley in memory of his little brother. The medley included a song by Justin's favorite contemporary Christian group, Tenth Avenue North, called "By Your Side," and "I Will Rise" by Chris Tomlin.

As my thoughts trailed back, I remember playing the CD in my car one day, and Justin said with excitement "Ma, that's my favorite group! Can I have that CD?" Of course, that became his CD.

I remember Donavan's melodious tones combined with Kelvin's masterful keyboard skills blended in a way that created a beautiful duo.

In addition, I would be hard-pressed to forget Justin's friend, Antonio. He has this story to share:

One night, several guys had gotten together in the dorm for vespers.

The song that they sung that evening was, "I Surrender All." It resonated with Justin in a deep and spiritual sense to the extent where he did not want to stop singing it. So, they sang that song over and over and over again, which lasted late into the night. Antonio expressed how Justin wished that he could sing like Antonio, who was an active member of the renowned Aeolians at the time. What was even more awe-inspiring was that Justin expressed his wish for Antonio to be the soloist at his wedding, and his funeral should he pass away before him.

That story gave me goosebumps, chills and produced more heart-wrenching tears. After hearing the story, the vocals that came after was nothing short of a work of art. To this day, that song moves me in a way that it never had before.

The service continued as Pastor Prince Lewis delivered the eulogy, and as I try to think back, the sermon is largely a blur. The casket, which contained a piece of my broken heart, was just a few feet in front of me. Have you ever had a dream that you just cannot remember the details about once you have awakened? The way that God created the brain is a beautiful thing. When reality becomes too much to accept or comprehend, the brain acts as a protective mechanism by partially shutting down. We can spontaneously dissociate to some degree from our surroundings, resulting in hidden memories.

However, one part of the eulogy that I do remember is the association of Justin's life as a punctuation mark. Pastor Prince Lewis made a comparison between a period and a comma, with Justin's life representing the latter. They are both punctuation marks, and yet the period denotes an end, while a comma indicates there is more to come. That was deep!

I'm unsure why but I recall the end of the service with much more clarity. There was a state-supported pathfinder presentation. Pathfinders are similar to Boy Scouts, but they are church-affiliated. I understand that it was the first time that this ceremony had been performed for a youth. They marched down the aisle and presented me with an American flag while my tears flowed. I could not bring myself to reach out and accept the flag because to accept the flag would mean I also accepted the reality that he was gone, and I was not ready to do that, even though I had a front-row seat in front of his coffin. My brave and loving son, Donavan, reached out and accepted the flag for me.

As everyone was marching out, the choir sang with both emotion and conviction. The song that I requested them to sing was "God Restores," made popular by a group called *Dynamic Praise*. It was so inspiring to me.

Sadly, my pain was immense, and my pathway looked dark, gloomy, and uncertain. However, I had enough faith to keep hope in Christ alive while keeping the coming day of restoration before me; the day that the "more to come" that follows the comma would be revealed. As I look back, this is the thread that helped me to maintain my sanity.

"For the Lord himself will come down from heaven with a commanding shout, with the voice of the archangel, and with the trumpet call of God. First, the believers who have died will rise from their graves. Then, together with them, we who are still alive and remain on the earth will be caught up in the clouds to meet the Lord in the air. Then we will be with the Lord forever. So encourage each other with these words."
(1 Thessalonians 4:16-18, NLT).

Chapter 10

The Aftermath

One definition of aftermath is "a period that follows an unpleasant event." That definition is far too tame to describe how I felt after the services. A more accurate, exclusive descriptive list would be words such as these: ruined, overwhelmed, dark, desolate, devastated, catastrophic, barren, and painfully empty.

Even though it was dark and difficult to see past my pain at that time, I knew that healing was possible because the Lord had brought me through several intimate losses. Though they were personal and painful, not one of them prepared me for the loss of my child. This time, I could not imagine healing; I could not see it; I could not feel it. The only thing that I could feel was the overwhelming sensation that this was the one that was designed to kill me both spiritually and physically.

Do you remember the nursery rhyme about Humpty Dumpty? The loss of my son was a great fall, and I did not know how, when, or if I would ever be pieced back together again. In the days that followed, I felt physically heavy, as if I had tripled in size. The most honest response I could make to "How do you feel?" was "I feel like I have been dragging cement blocks all night long and they are still with me."

I had never felt this way before in my entire life, which at times, caused me to question my sanity. Although there were a few people that I shared with, in general, these are not feelings that a person would be eager to reveal to others. The one that I continually cried out to was "God, Lord, have mercy on me! I don't understand or know how to sort out all of these emotions, but what I do know is that I need Your help!"

In addition, my short-term memory retention was ripped away from me. My friend, Vanessa, gave me a little book of brief devotions that I would read. However, as quickly as I read, the information was gone as if it had never happened. I had no idea what I had just read. I tried again and again and each time the same... no retention. It was as if my brain was a sieve and what was being poured into it was all filtering out, with no trace of content ever having been there. Can you imagine how frightening that was for me? As much as my heart was experiencing intense pain, it did not desensitize me to the fact that I needed God and His Word.

Therefore, instead of giving up, I repeated mantras that were short, simple, and powerful, such as... Jesus loves me. I also was inspired to write down scriptures that were short and simple, and I reviewed them regularly. I was really struggling and felt so unprepared for what was happening to me.

Fortunately, in the midst of chaos, the Holy Spirit helped me recall a commercial I saw years ago about depression. It illustrated a woman who was bent over from the weight of her emotional load. It was an unveiling moment for me as I realized... I am that woman... this is a heavy dose of depression. As I began to connect the dots, the picture became much clearer about what was happening to me; it was also quite clear that I would need much more help getting through my grief processing than ever before, and I was not ready for this challenge.

Granted, there are some challenges that we choose, such as a position with more responsibility and a higher salary. Personally, I find a whole lot of challenges on the golf course. However, I choose to keep going back over and over again. There are other situations that are handed to us by the circumstances of life and although we have the ability to make choices, it is Satan who is the ultimate cause and curator of all pain and suffering. In golf, what do you say when there's a wild golf ball flying through the air that might possibly injure someone? You yell "FORE!"

Sometimes I think it would be really, really, really great if there was a "shout out," a "heads up" that says "HEY! BRACE YOURSELF... CHALLENGES UP AHEAD..." Sometimes the challenge is that thing that comes out of left field... that comes seemingly out of nowhere and smacks you down like a worldwide wrestler. Sometimes it's not just any worldwide wrestler but a sumo wrestler who has jumped from a 20-foot platform and landed smack dab on your back. You then cannot imagine how you're *ever* going to recover from that! On the other hand, if we knew the details ahead of time and had time to absorb it all, most of us would worry ourselves literally to death. Sometimes it seems that life just isn't fair... and sometimes... it's just not.

The aftermath is a difficult place because it represents what is left after a devastating storm. There must be a clean-up process and even a triage process. What happens now? How do I move forward? I had so many questions and so few answers, which made me feel overwhelmed to the point of feeling stuck. In the meantime, Donavan was wrestling with his own personal aftermath journey.

"From the ends of the earth I call to you, I call as my heart grows faint; lead me to the rock that is higher than I." (Psalm 61:2, NIV)

Chapter 11

A Brother's Love

*T*ime is a continuous stream; it stops for no man. We each are granted an allotment of days, and for each of those days that we draw our breath, we borrow from the One who sustains us. From the inception of our origins, we are on borrowed time, and it is for each of us to seek out our purpose. I asked my phone for the definition of purpose and the result was, "The reason for which something is done or created or for which something exists."

It's a tall order, I'll admit, but it's our divine mandate to seek it out. The path our life takes is similar to a construction site. It is integral that we allow ourselves to reassess, rebuild, and reinvent ourselves along the way. Each step we take is the groundwork that molds us little by little.

Life is an adventure. It is a journey of constant change. From the moment that we are pushed forth from the birth canal, we embark on the quest of a lifetime. We are hurled into an unknown land, and we are being propelled toward a destination we do not know. We know nothing, rely on others for sustenance and our language is that of coos, shrieks, and blood-curdling screams. Life is the ultimate road trip, and we are all the passengers. There are pit stops, rest stops, unwarranted delays, accidents, roadblocks, and unforeseen hazardous conditions.

While we may all be on various road trips, each road trip is interconnected by a central theme: purpose. From the day we greet Mother Earth, we are all driven by the innate desire to find out what our purpose in life truly is.

As I contemplated that fact and how much I miss my little brother, my mind delved into the meaning of purpose, and what his life taught me about that notion. It taught me the things that are outlined below and so much more:

Pray About Everything

My earliest memories of my brother are when we went to the hospital on July 31, 1993. It was a Saturday night. I had spent the day at church with my grandparents, and my mind was all ablaze with excitement. It felt like that electric sensation a kid gets on Christmas morning when they wake up anticipating presents. It was a happy day for 5-year-old me; I finally had a little brother; he was an answer to my prayer.

Be Adventurous And Passionate

One thing I can say about my brother was that he was all for an adventure, and to him, life was one big mystery. It was his solemn duty to figure it out. He was going to figure it out and do it with 100 percent effort. I can't think of anyone else who had a zeal for life like Justin did.

One might wonder what it is like to have a sibling. Well, that all depends on who you ask. Some people have a love-hate relationship; some have no relationship; and some have that holiday "see ya once a year" relationship.

For me? It was like having your favorite annoying pest around. A very lovable and annoying pest who's also your best friend. Brothers share a unique experience. Arguments, laughs, and fun and games sum it up. More importantly, lots of love. Having a brother is having a partner in crime, a constant wrestling buddy, and a video game rival. Having a brother was like having a ready-made playmate. He might be an accomplice, and other times, an informant.

Justin was not one to back down from adversity. He was a "charge full-steam ahead" kind of guy. I recall one day after school, we were home by ourselves, and we had gotten into a tug of war of apocalyptic proportions. We were like gladiators in the Colosseum battling to the death, going blow for blow throughout the house for control of the remote.

We went at it for seemingly an eternity, but Justin was adamant. He would not give up his TV show. Even though I was five years his senior, he was not going to relent. Needless to say, he hit his head, and my will caved, and I handed over the remote. He was so mad that day, but in angry tones, he shouted, "Told you this would go my way."

Justin was tiny at this time, but he had a fire inside that was not to be reckoned with. Years later, we would laugh about this incident, but his unrelenting spirit transferred from the war of the remotes to the war for life.

Choose Your Battles
(Whenever Possible, Replace Conflict with Compassion.)

On one occasion, I remember we had gotten into an argument over the last bit of a box of cereal, of all things, and we started "fighting" in the hallway. During the altercation, Justin hit his head on the wall, and it wobbled like a bobblehead. I went into the apologetic big bro mode, and 15 minutes later, we were playing PS2 like nothing happened. I consider that a fond memory.

Be Persistent And Passionate

Justin was a big-time sports fan, but he was obsessed with gymnastics. And then there was me, the convenient cameraman. He was always trying to tumble off the top of the house onto a mattress placed strategically in the yard. He was always trying to perfect his back-handspring off the tree in the backyard. Day after day, he would go outside, tirelessly working on perfecting his craft. Whatever Justin was interested in, he was enthused and passionate about. His drive and enthusiasm are still intoxicating and a breath of fresh air for me today.

It's Okay To Spoil Your Baby Brother Sometimes

I admired him, so I did take the big brother privilege to spoil him. After my dad passed away, I made it a point to look out for him and make sure he was OK. Many times, I would get off work at 9 p.m. Justin was a student at Oakwood, and many nights, he would call me precisely at 9:05 p.m. like clockwork.

The conversation would begin with, "Bro, you know I love you, right?"

I would reply, "I love you too, but whatcha want, fool?"

And he would be like, "I'm hungry"

"Why didn't you go eat at the café, Justin?"

"I did. It was all nasty! You're gonna let your little brother starve? Can I have chicken nuggets and fries, please?"

He knew that I loved him and he had me wrapped around his little finger.

Life Can Be Harsh And Unpredictable

Life is very unpredictable; it's a new unwritten enigma every day. *The Lion King*'s song, "The Circle of Life," accurately depicts the constant change we undergo starting at birth.

My mind often wanders back to March 23, 2012. Like D-day, it will go down in infamy in the recesses of my mind. It was a Friday like any other Friday. I woke up, started my usual routine. I had a doctor's appointment, and afterward, I drove back to Oakwood's campus to meet up with Justin. I picked him up after class from Moran Hall, then we went to the market to grab some lunch before it closed.

We chit-chatted and talked about life. Justin was already asking for money for stuff he wanted to do that weekend, ha!

I drove him back to Holland Hall and was going to sign him out later that day, never knowing that would be the last time I would see my favorite knucklehead alive. Life is a very strange and unpredictable creature. This was 12 p.m. Come 3:20 p.m., I was getting a call that there had been an accident, and I should rush to the ER. I rushed out of my apartment as quickly as I received the call. Ever get that feeling in your gut and you just know that everything from here on out was about to be earth-shattering?

I didn't know what to expect as I broke every traffic law in Huntsville, racing to the hospital. I got to the hospital and it all feels surreal. *God? Not my brother! We just had lunch. He was full of life and in an upbeat spirit. This can't possibly be my life right now.*

I remember when this kid was born and all the times I prayed for a sibling. I remember he had gotten into some pills as a baby. I found him and let my parents know immediately, and that saved him. I was his big brother, his protector. I'm no stranger to the sting of death, having only lost our father less than four years prior. As painful as that was, this was different. My dad was terminally ill, whereas Justin was a healthy and happy-go-lucky college student. He was just reaching his prime. He was an adult, but your kid brother is always your kid brother. So often I rack my brain with what- ifs. Had I been there? Had I just taken him with me then… and so many other scenarios.

The medical staff was telling me that he didn't have a pulse, but they were able to get one, but he couldn't maintain it on his own. There have been a few times in life where I have prayed in earnest, hoping the outcome would change. All the while, I'm trying to process these thoughts. I didn't know what to tell my mom, who was currently a few states away. I wasn't ready to deal with that task. Around 5:05 p.m., doctors pronounced my brother dead, and at that moment, time stood still for me.

My 18-year-old little brother was gone. I asked if I could go into the room where they were keeping his body until the funeral home came to get him. I slowly opened the door, asked to be alone, and as I picked up my brother's lifeless, cold hand, I remembered the bear hug from hours ago. My phone went off, and as I reached in my pocket, there was the money I had already taken out of the ATM for him. I was shaken to my very core.

Time seems like such a trivial thing at times, and we often take it for granted. We always say things like "tomorrow," "it can wait," or "there is still time." To be honest, time is our most precious but fragile commodity. In our prime, we think we have all the time in the world; we feel invincible, and we waltz on with lackadaisical luster. Time is the metric by which we gauge our lives, and it's the tell-all by which we use the chances and opportunities afforded us.

Tomorrow is not promised; the next minute is not either. Life is meant for living, not merely existing. At the time I'm writing this, it is the sixth birthday Justin will never see. He would be 24, a man in his own right. I can imagine how he would be spending today. He was all about living and not simply existing. I imagine he would wanna go do something action-packed, like skydiving or bungee jumping. It's a crazy notion for my brain to compute that he isn't here. There's not a day that I don't miss my little brother and best friend. He definitely was a breath of fresh air to all he came in contact with. Justin Hanna was many things, but his most notable trait was that "people are people," and he treated every soul he met as such.

I can't think of anyone else who had a zeal for life like Justin did.

Work hard, play hard and love hard — those were prevailing themes in his life.

Justin also had a few temporary setbacks, but he didn't let that stop him; he pushed ahead full force. Giving up was not in his vocabulary. Justin's purpose was to seize life's opportunities and maximize them. Whether it was extreme physical feats or standing up for those less fortunate, he didn't want to let one moment slip by him. Justin was a philosopher at heart, and as he matured into manhood, his context for purpose expanded and showed in his daily transformation.

He discovered that not only is our purpose to seize every opportunity life has to offer us, but more importantly, that his purpose was to live out his life to the extreme as he lived it for his Maker. He connected the dots that our greatest purpose resides in our relationship with God.

Persevere "Until Then"

There's not a day that goes by that I don't miss him, not a day that I wish I could see the kind of man he would be right now; not a day goes by that my heart doesn't feel the void of his absence, but as the song sung so beautifully by T. Marshall Kelly says,

> "My heart can sing when I pause to remember,
> A heartache here is but a stepping stone,
> Along a path that's always winding upward,
> This troubled world is not my final home,
> But until then, my heart will go on singing.
> Until then, with joy I'll carry on.
> Until the day my eyes behold that city.
> Until the day God calls me home."

However painstaking it may be in life to press on, we must remember that this life is our transition, not our final destination. I often must remind myself of that when my mind is washed by the waves of grief and despair, "*until then.*"

Sometimes, as believers, we forget we have a blessed hope and great expectancy that rings loud and true amidst the sorrow. The hollowed words of Jesus on the cross, that ring down the corridors of eternity. "It is finished."

One day, the final nail will be driven into the coffin of this bleak sin afflicted world, but, "until then."

Chapter 12

How to Move Forward When Your Feet Are Stuck in Cement

*F*or me, there was a desire to move forward emotionally, and yet I could not because I felt as if my feet were stuck in cement. There was a plethora of unanswered questions bombarding my mind, along with a menagerie of emotions that many times conflicted with each other. I agonized with God over these thoughts that I could not silence. How did this happen? Why did this happen? God, I know that You could have saved him; why didn't You?

After the loss of my late husband, I spent some time in physical and emotional recuperation at Wildwood Lifestyle Center because the last six weeks of his life, in particular, were very traumatic and my nerve endings needed to be nurtured and soothed. Remarkably, just being in that environment, surrounded by nature with the doctors and attendants who prayed with me before each process was relaxing and very comforting. This time, I felt stuck, and initially was not sure what I should do.

What I did know is that I did not want to be away from home alone and with a group of strangers. Oh Lord, what should I do? What about my job? How could I focus on work? All of these bombarding thoughts and feelings contributed to this awful monolithic feeling of being weighed down.

The answer to the perplexing question of what I should do eventually came to me, but it was not the answer that I expected. At that particular period, the main thing was to stand still and keep praying. Outside of taking care of my daily needs and basic responsibilities, that was all that I could do, and yet I wanted more. I continued to feel drained, as if I had been performing continual manual labor and there was a love/hate relationship with sleep. It was very much needed and yet sleep was the enemy because when I slept, I would often have very vivid dreams of my baby.

I remember one dream that was particularly disturbing because Justin was standing in front of me and as I reached out to hug him, anticipating one of his great big warm bear hugs that he always gave me, instead, he felt so very, very cold. I woke up uncovered and shivering while realizing that it was all just a dream, which brought on a massive flood of uncontrollable tears. I continued to wonder when or if I would be released from this bonded state — to feel at least somewhat normal again and move forward in my unwanted grief journey. When would I feel better?

As I continued to pray and tried to look for light out of this darkness, I realized that although Donavan lived eight hours away, speaking with him daily was extremely helpful to me, and I strived to encourage him as well. Also, the support of family and close friends proved to be a blessing too and was very much appreciated. These intimate relationships never lost their value. However, the knife in my heart continued to twist, while creating the most excruciating pain that I have ever felt in my entire life.

It felt as if I was bleeding profusely and there was no clotting factor in sight. As my mind continued to look for words to describe this unwanted and unnatural feeling, I realized that combined with the excruciating pain is a deep sense of emptiness because there is a gaping hole where a part of my heart used to be. Have you ever been so hurt and disappointed about the result of a situation that your heart just does not want to believe? There was a battle going on between what I wanted to be so... and a reality I did not want to accept. My heart was shattered, broken into too many pieces to count. Who wants to believe that a parent's worst nightmare is now a reality?

It's possible to empathize, but difficult to really relate unless you have actually walked in these shoes, and even then, grief is a very customized, personal journey. What I can tell you, though, is that I felt as though I was stuck in an emotional vat of cement and could not see my way out. How could I move forward with my feet stuck in cement?

It took some time for me to come to a point of self-reasoning. Although, I was functioning and looked progressive on the outside, internally, I was in a fog for what seemed like months. The more time passed, and I could not speak with him, see him, or hug him, the more it hurt, and it seemed like nothing could fill that emptiness. As I look back, I really don't know where hurt ended and anger began, but I felt that at some point, these two emotions just somehow blended together.

Unfortunately, like Mary and Martha when their brother died in John 11, I was at a place, calling, "Lord... if You had just been here. Lord... if You... had... just... been here, my child would not have died. Lord... where were You?"

Additionally, there was Job, who felt injustices were done to him and wanted God to show him where he had done anything wrong deserving of his tragedies. (Job 38) There are two points that come to mind here.

First, when tragedies happen, it is not necessarily due to anything that we have personally done. Secondly, it is human to resist the impact of hardships and even ask questions. I did not know how to engage with my emotions, nor did I want to learn, because it was just too painful. I was confused and conflicted regarding my thoughts and emotions.

Some of those conflicting thoughts included identifying God as the cause of my loss. I never doubted that He is all-knowing and all-powerful, but there was a part of me that was blaming Him because He did not stop the incident from happening. Sometimes there would be situations that would cause disturbing thoughts, such as when someone's child would be miraculously saved. I would wonder, "Why not my child?"

Other times, the thought would come regarding teenagers who were disrespectful to their parents and who did not give their mothers great big bear hugs like Justin gave to me and they were still walking around, still being disrespectful.

Oh, I was happy for the miracles and for the opportunities for the disrespectful to become respectful, but still, there was that awful longing to be reconnected with my child.

My thoughts and conversations with God continued. "Lord, he was so excited about his internship that was coming up in the summer and about being focused on his studies. He was excited about his future and his relationship with You. Lord, he had selected a stack of books from his grandmother's storage that he wanted to read over the summer."

As I looked through the box, I found a diverse collection of books covering topics from American history to psychology; from classics, to culture, to romance, to adventure. Some of the titles included:

A Day in the Life of President Kennedy
Evangeline, by Henry Wadsworth Longfellow
Roots, by Alex Haley
A Raisin in the Sun, by Lorraine Hansberry
Voyage to The Bottom of the Sea, by Raymond Jones

Why God? Why did this have to happen? Why now? At this point, I was not angry, but hurt beyond measure, and I just wanted a list of things to do to take away the excruciating pain and emptiness. I really wanted to move forward, but how?

Seemingly, there are those who find returning to work to be very helpful in similar circumstances. However, that was not true in my case because the very thought of it produced nightmares. One of my biggest fears was returning to work and being asked how I was coping, when truthfully, that was a question that many times even I could not answer. A part of me wanted to be able to put on a brave face and say, "I'm good by God's Grace," but that would have been a lie.

Therefore, as I look back, I do not take it lightly that the Lord impressed upon my manager's heart to be patient with me rather than pressure me to return to work. My supervisor and managers were very supportive and assured me that I did not have to worry about my job and that I could take as much time as I needed. How often does that happen? What a huge blessing! Those words were like life-giving oxygen being pumped through my lungs and the beginning of the process needed to chip away at the cement that seemed to bind me.

Although, at the time, my pain kept me from clearly seeing God's mercy, one day He metaphorically provided my very own *Beer- Lahai- Roi* in the privacy of my bathroom. According to Strong's Concordance, that is the Hebrew name which means "The well where the Living God sees me." My bathroom! Who goes to the bathroom to find spiritual revelation? This was life-changing for me as I stood there staring into my bathroom mirror. This ordinary place was mysteriously transformed from its common purpose into a Holy meeting place.

This experience was both unexpected and monumental for me as I stood there, blankly staring into the mirror on the wall. You may wonder what was holding my attention there. I can assure you it was not my disheveled appearance that I was focused on.

Have you ever been staring at something, and you saw it, but really did not see it because your mind was focused on something that was so much bigger than what's seen in the mirror? That is exactly what happened. I had an unexpected encounter with God through the Holy Spirit. He revealed to me a path that would take me from being cemented in hurt and negative emotion to a place of moving forward with the awareness of divine help. He introduced me to His plan for my life through a "Call to Arms."

"I will instruct you and teach you the way that you should go; I will counsel you with my eye upon you." (Psalm 32:8 ESV)

Chapter 13

The Call To Arms

*T*he phrase "Call to Arms" has several definitions. The one that applies to my situation is this one found in the Merriam-Webster online dictionary: "a summons, invitation, or appeal to undertake a particular course of action." As the conversation continued, the appeal was given.

"Child, it is time for you to get up."

I continued to stare into the mirror while conversing with Him who began to reveal Himself to me in a way I had not experienced before. Little did I realize in that instant that the Holy Spirit was also slowly pulling back my emotional layers so that I could see myself with clarity.

While we talked, the Holy Spirit spoke to me with such gentleness, patience, understanding, and love in spite of the charges against me. I had been charged with "Mistaken Identity." It was not my identity that had been mistaken but God's identity. God has always known me and loved me to the extent that He has written my name in the palm of His hands. (Isaiah 49:16) I was the one who inflicted the mistaken identity upon Him. For some, this statement may be a bit confusing. So, let's delve further into this idea of "mistaken identity."

The essence of mistaken identity is inaccurately identifying or associating an innocent person as the culprit. Let us consider this question: How often does God get blamed for the horrid things that happen in our world? Think about it. When there is property damage as a result of a storm, it is referred to as "an act of God." I want to reiterate, when my baby passed away, I identified God as the cause of my loss. Without hesitation, I acknowledged Him as both all-powerful and all-knowing; here, my thoughts were quite accurate. However, there was an internal conflict created by also entertaining the thought of playing the blame game with God because He did not intervene in the way that I wanted Him to. Ironically, at the time, I did not even realize this is what I was doing because there were so many emotions and so many thoughts that were going on in my head.

So, there I stood, guilty before God. And today, I am both amazed and forever grateful to Him because He could have said, "What do you think you're doing, young lady? How dare you have these emotions and ask me these questions!" Instead of an abrupt retort to my pain and doubt, He responded ever so gently. Instead of striking me down, He accepted me as the broken, contrite soul that I was, and patiently allowed me to go through the various stages of loss. According to Dr. Kuebler Ross, there are seven stages: shock, denial, anger, bargaining, depression, testing, and acceptance. The first six happened to me in cyclical waves, and acceptance was a long and unwanted journey.

Our bathroom reconciliation continued with, "My child, remember what has long been one of your favorite verses? 'Trust in the Lord with all of your heart and do not depend on your own understanding' (Proverbs 3:5, NLT). Vanessa, the One that you are so angry with is your only source of healing and restoration. I am the way."

This gentleness was like a refreshing breeze on a hot summer day, and His timing was simply impeccable. Then, when the fullness of time had come, the Holy Spirit brought to the surface that which had been covered up under pain and agony: acknowledgment of my deep need and desire to be restored to Christ.

I wonder if I could be any more thankful for Him looking way beyond my faults and addressing my needs with so much love. My humble, heartfelt response was... "Yes Lord. You are right. You are my only hope for healing and restoration. I love You, and I am so sorry that I ever doubted You and even blamed You. Please forgive me."

Do you know anyone who has ever felt this way? Do not be so quick to say "no," because chances are you know them, but they may never openly admit it. Instead, those emotions remain bottled up inside and they potentially become the angriest person sitting on the church board who rarely agrees with anything. If we confess our sins, He is faithful and just to forgive us our sins and to cleanse us from all unrighteousness. (1 John 1:9)

At this point in the conversation, I was convicted and fully aware that I was both guilty and forgiven. It was only after confession and surrender that I could now receive my "Call to Arms." God reminded me that the blood of Jesus is sufficient and gave me His shoulder to cry on while encouraging me to cast all of my burdens on Him (1 Peter 5:7) because His shoulders are big enough, strong enough, loving enough to bear my burdens.

Granted, I was not the first person, and I am certain that I will not be the last to have experienced doubt, but I sure felt like I was one of the most remorseful. Quite honestly, had I been able to place things in the proper perspective from the beginning, I would have shouted, "An enemy has done this!"

God is not the enemy. Who is the enemy? That title belongs to Satan. When he speaks, he speaks in his slithery, lying, native tongue and has well earned his title, *"The Father of Lies"* (John 8:44). He is a formidable foe, but also a defeated one because in the end, Jesus wins! (Revelation 20:10)

The truth of the matter is, God loves humanity so much that He gave us choice and a tree, and we know how that turned out, don't we? Adam and Eve chose to listen to Satan rather than God in Genesis 3, and the end result was and is sin, pain, and death until the appointed time when death will be no more, and all tears are wiped away. (Revelation 21:4)

Grief does not come in a "one size fits all" package because it is such a personal journey. This is true both for each person and each loss. Think about it: we do not grieve in the same way and intensity for every loss. Therefore, when the time was right for me, God made it known to me through His Holy Spirit that it was time to begin looking from the natural to the spiritual in order to continue the process of moving forward from the things that bound and confounded me.

He laid out the plan that would move me forward in His strength and under the protective shadow of His wings. His plan for me was uniquely designed to bring me comfort, healing, and to save me from myself. Furthermore, it would provide a ministry platform to help reach others for Christ.

As the conversations continued, the appeal was reinforced, "My child, it is time for you to listen very carefully because I have a mission that can only be carried out by you. In essence, Vanessa, this mission, should you choose to accept it, is to share your story and declare My Glory."

What? Share my story? Have you ever been in a situation where you were convicted to straighten up and fly right, and before you know it, here comes a test? I found this assignment to be a little intimidating because the first thing that comes to mind is that my story is about the death of my child. That's a morbid story, and I really don't want to talk about that over and over again. Isaiah 41:13 came to life right in front of me: *"For I am the Lord your God who takes hold of your right hand and says to you, do not fear. I will help you."*

Although the assignment is intimidating, my commitment to carrying it out while totally depending on God was undaunted. In addition, the Holy Spirit helped me to say that my story is more than the death of a child. It is about setting the record straight. It is about declaring the Glory of God to the world! Praise God! I was again convicted, and my response was "OK God, with Your help, I will accept as many opportunities as You provide to do what You have asked me to do."

Many times, I have heard others refer to God as a "Gentleman who does not force us to do anything." This means we always have a choice to accept or reject Him and His call. My mission is to tell as many people as I can that

God is not the enemy; to tell as many people as I can that God is not the least bit indifferent regarding our pain, because not only did God suffer for us on the cross, but He embraces us and suffers with us when we are hurting (Hebrews 4:15) to declare God's Glory. What is God's Glory?

In Exodus 33, Moses wanted to know more on this topic as well. He asked God to show him His Glory. He was saying to God, "Show me your character, your essence so that I might know you even better." Now, that was a larger-than-life request. Apparently, Moses had developed a relationship so close with God that He felt like he could ask Him absolutely anything. As Christians, we have that same bonding opportunity that Moses had.

I wonder if it is that same bond that inspired Paul to write "...*with Thanksgiving, let your requests be made known to God*"? (Philippians 4:6) Our relationship with God should be just that close. So, what was the answer to the question? The answer came in Exodus 34:6: "*And he passed in front of Moses, proclaiming, 'The Lord, the Lord, the compassionate and gracious God, slow to anger, abounding in love and faithfulness.'*"

Yes, God's Glory is His character. He has no desire to win our love by the strength of His greatness but by the strength of His character. On this earth, we may never understand His wisdom, but we simply must trust His will. My personal proclamation is that my eyes have seen the Glory of the Lord! Yes, He is compassionate, gracious, slow to anger, loving, and faithful! It is because of Him that I went through this dark period and came out on the other side with my sanity and my testimony intact. *Oh, magnify the Lord, for He is worthy to be praised!* (Psalms 145:3)

He continues to be my strength on days when the weight of loss and life gets too heavy. So, you see, God is not just loving, but the purest form of love that can be found anywhere. (1 John 4:8) How deep is His love? It is unfathomable. Love is an action word. Jesus left His heavenly kingdom to come to this world, where He suffered and died a cruel, painful death. Why? So that we would have the opportunity to be restored and live with Him eternally. Hallelujah! Praise God!

And after this experience and acknowledging all of this about God, how can I not love a God like that? He is *El Roi*, the God who sees me! To be seen by the God of the universe is awesome! To be seen is to be known, to be known, is to be accepted in spite of my faults, and to be accepted is to be unconditionally loved.

God accepted me, and I accepted the mission. Trust me: moving forward was not an overnight process for me, but I had to continue the process of *busting out* of that cement. So, the next step is to put the mission in action, carrying out the "call to arms" and moving forward.

"You will show me the path of life." (Psalm 16:11, NKJV)

Chapter 14

My Faith Walk Through the Shadow of Death

*I*really wanted to live this mission, but I recognized that was not going to be easy. Why? Because my heart was (and is) still hurting. I learned that when times are hard, it is important to have something deep inside that will motivate you to fight the urge to quit. Let me share with you some of what was deep inside that kept me going even while tears were flowing.

First of all, I cannot overemphasize the importance of having a personal relationship with Christ *prior* to devastation. One of the functions of the Holy Spirit is to help us to recall God's Word. (John 14:26) "Recall means to remember something that you previously knew." Unfortunately, there can be no recall from a blank slate. However, if you do not have a relationship with God prior to tragedy, all is not lost. Even then, if you come to God in faith, He is willing to forgive and help you. (Psalm 86:5)

By faith, I knew that my life had purpose, and if I did not know it prior to my bathroom becoming my *beer-lahai-roi*, then I certainly knew it afterward. I had been called by God to do this thing that was so much bigger than me, and historically, that is what God does. He calls us to do things that will help us to recognize Him as our ultimate resource and refuge. He did not call Moses to divide a puddle but a Red Sea. This kept me going forward.

Secondly, it was important for me to acknowledge and accept that no one else can fulfill my mission. I have to tell my own story for four reasons. 1) Because God said so; 2) To help myself recall God's presence in the midst of my trial; 3) So that I could be a blessing to other parents who have lost children; 4) Because no one else can tell my personal experience like I can. This kept me going.

Thirdly, my son, Donavan, loves and needs me. Although he was assisting in the role of comforter, supporter, and protector, he was hurting too. It's not easy to lose your father and your brother before graduating from college. There was a lot going on, but that still, small voice was saying "Get up child! It's time for your breakthrough." This kept me going forward.

So, you see: God brought me into the realization of who He is. Who is God?

God is not just loving, but God IS love, and yes, He is all-powerful! However, He did not just say "Boom. Healed. You're good to go." Instead, He took me on a faith walk through the shadow of death. He took me through a process. We do not always understand His plan, but we must trust and believe that Jesus is the Good Shepherd and will never lead us astray. (John 10:11) Although I was continually praying along with many family members and friends, I was in a scary place in my life. However, with all of the courage that could be mustered, I desperately wanted to follow God wherever He was leading me and embrace the gentle nudge to get up. After all, James 2:17 (NLT) tells me, "*Faith without works is dead.*"

The process was not fully revealed to me all at once but through the guidance of the Holy Spirit. At various intervals, the plan was unveiled. If you are someone who has experienced a tragedy, please let me encourage you by sharing with you actions that helped and continue to help me. I am sharing this information because I want to be a blessing to all those who have been devastated by loss, who knows someone that you would like to help, and especially to those who have experienced the loss of a child and may still be struggling with this phenomenon that Paul refers to as "*the last enemy to be destroyed*" (1 Corinthians 15:26).

I pray that these actions that helped me and continue to be a source of healing for me will be helpful in your situation as well. So, continue on this journey with me as I reveal my path to restoration and healing. Let us explore these steps together.

The process involved the following areas: Spiritual, Mental/Emotional, Physical, and Social.

1. Spiritual

In order to get to this point in my faith journey, it was necessary for me to be willing to look through spiritual eyes to see and appreciate the positive.

1. My son was not on drugs or associated with a gang.
2. Spiritually/educationally, his head/heart was in the right place. I will never forget the breaking news headline, "Oakwood University Freshman Who Drowned Was 'Spiritually Focused.'"
3. On that same day, he had lunch on campus with his brother.
4. We had a great relationship. Our last words on that very day were "I love you."

If you are feeling like God cannot be trusted, I appeal to you to be willing to learn to trust again. Jesus is the best Friend that we can ever have, and the only means of hope and healing. When in doubt, repeat

John 3:16. *"For God so loved the world, that He gave His only begotten son..."*

The Power of an Active Prayer Life

Pray without ceasing. (1 Thessalonians 5:17)

There were so many people praying for me and our family. People all across the United States, as well as internationally. Justin had a friend from Korea who had spread the word to his family there and asked for them to share our great loss with others so that they too could join in prayer on our behalf. People were praying for me when I did not even know they were praying. Those prayers were especially crucial for me during times when the weight of my loss felt unbearable. There is power in prayer and meditating on God's Word.

Additionally, I was also praying for myself and sometimes the only prayer I could muster was, "Oh God, please help me." I talked to Him about the things that I liked as well as the things that I was not happy about. What would I have gained to try to hide how I felt from God besides a relationship built on pretense? Relationships cannot grow and develop in the way that they need to when pretense is at the center.

The Power of God's Word

"Trust in the LORD with all of your heart and lean not to your own understanding." (Proverbs 3:5)

I have a dear friend who shares the same first name as me, Vanessa. She was inspired to give me a little devotional book that is small enough to fit in the palm of my hand. This book contained bite-sized devotional readings that I could attempt to digest. In the beginning, even those small plates of scriptural food proved to be too much for my emotionally devastated mind to retain.

Although it was a little overwhelming, I kept trying. Later, I realized that focusing on a favorite mantra, such as, "Though I walk through the valley of the shadow of death, I will hold on to God's hand, knowing that He is walking with me and strengthening me." Even reading one or two words and meditating on that, along with what I could recall from previous study, was comforting and reassuring. Sometimes I would listen to the recorded Word. Listening, hearing, and reading are a powerful combination. (Revelation 1:3)

In Philippians 4:11, Paul shares how he learned to be content in all circumstances. When Jesus was in the Garden of Gethsemane, that was not a happy time for Him, and He definitely was not jumping up and down in joyful glee. There were many days when trusting in what I could not see was an agonizing faith walk but I have learned that being content does not necessarily mean being happy about what happened. It does mean trusting God to walk with you through whatever your trial may be. I am a living witness that the scriptures testify of God and His love. Also, they have the power to bring you hope, healing, and restoration. (John 5:39)

Encouraging Passages

I encourage you to meditate on these scriptures as well as others included in this book. Repeat them over and over again until you and them become one. You may have some other favorites because the Bible includes a vast wealth of comfort and wisdom.

2 Samuel 22:29 (NIV) *"You are my lamp, O Lord; the Lord turns my darkness into light."*

Psalms 55:22 (NLT) *"Give your burdens to the Lord and He will take care of you."*

Philippians 4:19 (KJV) *"But my God will supply all your need according to his riches in glory by Christ Jesus."*

Hebrews 4:16 (NIV) *"Let us then approach God's throne of grace with confidence, so that we may receive mercy and find grace to help us in our time of need."*

Psalms 23:4 (NKJV) *"Yea, though I walk through the valley of the shadow of death, I will fear no evil; For you are with me; Your rod and Your staff, they comfort me."*

2. Mental/Emotional

Memories

Happy memories can be very healing as we reflect on them. Our memories are those cherished experiences that seem to touch us in the depths of our hearts and soul. The kind that makes us almost feel the warmth of a hug. They can make us laugh and sometimes release a salty tear. They are precious, priceless images and emotions because we will never be able to produce any new ones. Although I've shared some in previous chapters, here are a few more of my favorite memories:

One cold night in Huntsville, Alabama, Donavan had taken Justin and some of his friends to a store, and outside of the store was a homeless woman. Justin proceeded to take his coat off and give it to the woman as his friends urged him not to because it was his favorite coat. Instead, they urged pooling together to buy her a blanket. His response was profound. "Unless you give something that you really want, it's really not giving."

He marched against Alabama's HB56 law, which was then known as one of the harshest anti-immigration laws in the nation. He did not have any relatives that were immigrants; there was no personal gain to be achieved. What he did have was a desire to help those less fortunate.

Justin's High School class at Mount Pisgah Academy, lead by Andrew Grissom did something that touched my heart to tears. They created the Justin Hanna Scholarship in his memory. In addition, there is a dedication emblem on the class's stunning, rock formation water fountain on campus. It reads, class of 2011, in memory of Justin Hanna. To know that he was so much loved, respected honored makes me feel extra proud and thankful to God.

On the weekend of what would have been his Oakwood University Graduation, he surprisingly became an Honorary Graduate. His picture and graduation sash were draped upon a chair seated amongst the other graduates. It was emotional, thoughtful, and beautiful. In addition, I had an opportunity to speak at the Parent/Senior Reception with an audience of approximately 700 class members and families. My heart beams as my mind travels back to that very special day. Even now, I'm excited. Do you know why? I was able to share memories and one of my favorite stories about the Christmas gift Justin gave to me — the perfume. My message theme and charge to the class was "Three Squirts." The crux of my message:

For success and the pursuit of true happiness, all you need is three continuous squirts of God the Father, God the Son, and God the Holy Spirit. Three squirts. So, I said to the class of 2015: move forward, pursue the dreams that God has placed in your hearts and be truly blessed. It was a very fulfilling moment.

These are all memories that I don't ever want to forget because they inspire me to strive to be better. Because we are human, by default, the law of diminishing returns is enacted. In general, as time passes, our memories are not as photostatic as they used to be. What can we do? Write down as many thoughts and memories as we share our stories. Share their stories. The very practice of writing sharpens each impression. Before you know it, you may have a book to publish. Share your story!

Christian Counseling

The Bible speaks of wise counsel.

Proverbs 11:14 (NKJV) *"Where there is no counsel, the people fall; But in the multitude of counselors there is safety."*

Proverbs 20:18 (NASB) *"Prepare plans by consultation ..."*

Proverbs 12:15 (NKJV) *"The way of a fool is right in his own eyes, But he who heeds counsel is wise."*

In all honesty, I am convinced that all pastors are not equipped to provide effective grief counseling. It has been my experience that possessing a gift to preach like Paul does not automatically place that same person into the category of gifted grief counselor. However, I am ultra-grateful to the Lord for intervening on my behalf in order to connect me with a pastor who is endowed with skills of Christian counseling.

I have to give God total praise because this pastor was located more than 300 miles from where I live. Therefore, I would have never even considered him. He had a pretty full schedule since he pastored a very large church in Atlanta, Georgia. But God knew just what I needed, and He knew how to make it happen.

The Holy Spirit convicted him to create time to meet with me weekly. We would get on the phone, sometimes as early as 6:30 in the morning, to meet for prayer and counsel for a brief period of time. In addition, as a part of one of his sermons, he gave me a platform to tell my story of beauty and pain. As I think back on that time, I will always be grateful to that wise and kind man of God.

Professional Christian Counseling

In my journey to restoration, the Lord led me to seek professional counseling in addition to the brief pastoral counseling that I received. I prayerfully searched for a Christian counselor. For me, it took meeting with at least three different counselors before making a final decision. Often, there are those who are opposed to this kind of assistance because some equate it with being faithless. My personal view is if I can schedule an appointment with a medical doctor to assist with my physical concerns, then I can certainly make an appointment to discuss my emotional well-being because both can be traumatic and painful.

I had to do this for myself. I encourage anyone who feels led to get professional counseling to do so without accepting other's judgment of you. This time is really not about them but about you and your recovery. When things around you feel bigger and taller than you are, you must do what you need to do in order to get unstuck... to get out of the cement and move forward.

Choosing to Be Victorious Over Negative Self-Talk

Numerous studies and articles show that women are more likely to participate in negative self-talk than men. This realization was and is very empowering to me because it causes me to be more aware of what I say to myself. When I noticed some of my conversations with myself included phrases such as "I will never get through this," I could then turn it around to say something such as, "This is the most painful situation that I have ever experienced, but I can do all things through Christ who strengthens me."

When the voice in your head says you're in too deep this time and you will never make it... you'll never be successful... you will never get through this... do not listen to it! Instead, take every thought captive (2 Corinthians 10:5) and repeat the information in a way that is truthful, strengthening, and empowering to help you persevere.

Support Groups

Even after I had meetings with the pastor and a counselor, I found that there was something still missing from a support perspective. Although nurturing by family and close friends is very important, many times, there may be members of these groups who simply do not understand your journey. My support group was vitally important. It included my son, Donavan, close friends of Justin, family members, co-workers, and friends.

Eventually, a friend suggested meeting with others who have similar experiences. Initially, I was hesitant, but this turned out to be a beautiful experience for me. I can now describe a good support group of shared experiences as being like the embryonic fluid that gently surrounds the unborn fetus to facilitate growth and provide protection. I met with a couple of different groups, and it was very liberating for me. Why? Because within these groups, I had permission to openly grieve in a non-judgmental environment. Grieving people need to have permission and time to grieve in their own unique ways.

I mentioned this previously but find this a good place to reiterate. Among some Christians, there is a reluctance to seek professional counseling or participate with groups such as these because of the stigma of faithlessness that is often, in my opinion, inaccurately associated. I recently met a Christian counselor who shared that there are a multitude of untreated mental health issues in the church. I found that comment to be very revealing and aligned with some of the conversations that I have had with grieving people.

Speak Out

I placed speaking out under the umbrella of mental/emotional because although there are moments that are more challenging than others, in general, sharing my story is medicinal in a manner that is physically, mentally, and emotionally beneficial. When I speak to audiences, whether it is one or 700, it is a healing experience for at least two simple reasons: 1) I am fulfilling my mission; 2) When I help others, it makes me feel good too.

The Holy Spirit used my desire to help others, to inspire me to speak with a member of management, to gain approval to begin a grief ministry on campus where I worked at the time. This was uncharted waters, since a group such as this had never existed in our workplace. Remarkably, the response was favorable, and the group met quarterly and even received financial support from the company. Wow! God is nothing short of amazing!

The largest group that I have shared with so far has been a crowd of approximately 700. I would have been fearful, but God remembered me and said, "*Do not fear, I will help you*" (Isaiah 41:13). I trusted Him — for He is not man; He does not lie (Numbers 23:19) — and instead of being fearful, I felt empowered, energized, and recommitted to speak wherever He leads. To God be the glory!

That was not the only opportunity. I have had many opportunities to speak on women's prayer lines, Women's Day church events, Women's Retreat seminars, and I presented a "How to Get Started with Grief Ministry in your Church" for the South Atlantic Conference of Seventh Day Adventist.

Speaking out through written communications is another area that allows me to simultaneously be expressive and heal, which is why I am writing this book. Prior to this book, journaling was my original life flow. It was the mechanism that reminded me of joys and provided a form of release when situations were stressful and could not be shared with another human being. As I think about this now, journaling was actually my preparation platform for the speaking and writing that I am doing today. Eventually, I started a blog called "From Nightfall to Morning Light." I chose that name because nightfall is where I was, but my sights were set on what I call the "morning light" phase. I think of the morning light phase as a period of renewal and refreshing. It reminds me of Psalm 46:5: "*God is in the midst of her... God will help her when morning dawns.*"

In addition, I have written articles for entities such as *Message Magazine,* *She Magazine,* and *Southern Tidings* that incorporate various pieces of my personal grief journey and how God holds my hand through the process.

3. The Physical

Through my journey, the Lord reawakened my senses to the direct connection between the physical and the mental/emotional. If you're depressed, your body says, "I am too." Remember, earlier I shared that in the early days after the loss of my child, my body felt heavy, as if I had been carrying a load of bricks on my back or cement in my feet? The emotional stress launched a physical attack. What helped me tremendously from a physical and mental perspective is the intentional spiking of endorphins. Many of us describe endorphins as the "feel good" hormones. Although endorphins are produced in our bodies, they can be triggered through laughter and through exercise.

Many years ago, I read a very interesting article about a man named Norman Cousins, who was challenged with a very painful illness. Amazingly, he found that time spent in laughter resulted in at least a couple of hours of pain reduction. Even more incredulous is that thousands of years before Norman Cousin's discovery, Solomon in his wisdom had already discovered that *"A cheerful heart is good medicine, but a crushed Spirit dries up the bones"* (Proverbs 17:22). Like Solomon and Norman, among others, I am also a witness to the fact that laughter really does help you feel better emotionally and physically.

Walking was the other activity that helped propel me out of the dark space that I was occupying. I found walking through a wooded area to be so peaceful and comforting. There was just something about being in nature that was both attractive and healing for me. I would either call a friend to go with me or I would walk in an area that was frequented with other walkers. It may require digging deeper than you think you can go, but for anyone trying to climb out of a challenging situation, I would recommend prayerfully finding a way to create endorphins every day.

When talking about the importance of taking care of our physical needs on the road to healing and recovery, for me, having a healthy plant-based diet could not be overlooked as a healing agent contributor. I remember speaking with Dr. Richard Berry, who shared that studies show that a person is 21 times more likely to have a heart attack within 24 hours of the loss of a close loved one. I thought, "WOW." I had no idea, but I can clearly see how that could occur.

I believe that my plant-based diet helped with strengthening my heart muscles, keeping my arteries clear, and even helped me from sinking into a much more extensive episode of depression. Drs. Ned Nedley and T. Colin Campbell, among others, believe that a well-balanced, plant-based diet can enhance all areas of our physical and mental health. I definitely believe that it had a positive impact on my recovery.

I had to make sure I was eating in a way that was balanced. This was the tricky part because when you're grieving, you don't always feel like preparing food and eating. This is one reason I feel that it's a great idea and service, to at least supply the grieving household with meals for at least a couple of months; longer if possible.

Although creating balance is particularly easier said than done during times of grief, it is an essential element. In the beginning, there was food prepared for me by various people and brought to my home. When that ended, I had to create enough balance in my life to make sure that my self-preservation side was up and running effectively. After all, it would be difficult to fulfill my mission while my body was only running on fumes. So, I returned to juicing and eating balanced meals. A good night's sleep remained difficult for a while, but eventually, that too came to fruition and was very much needed.

Social

It was important for me to be selective about those who I allowed to be in my inner circle. I cannot emphasize enough the importance of being surrounded by people who are supportive and positive. Distancing, if not eliminating, may be necessary for those who do not show themselves to be positive and supportive. Again, if you feel led to do so, you have the option to place them in a "to be continued" category for a time, realizing they are only helpful in certain situations. I did not view this as being mean, and you should not either. Instead, I see it as a natural, drug-free antibiotic used to facilitate the healing process by eliminating those things that can *"crush the spirit and dry up the bones"* (Proverbs 17:22).

Incidentally, I learned that it was perfectly fine to have what I call "Nessa time," which is time alone with my thoughts and feelings while not ruling out being social. In the beginning, I felt guilty about socializing and resuming "fun" activities because somehow, it felt as if I was moving on and leaving my baby behind. Grief is an individual journey, and it took some time for me to realize and accept that I could not effectively function while remaining in a place where the pain was so intense. Instead of thinking of it as leaving Justin behind, I needed to think of it as finding a new normal while forever carrying the good memories with me.

Therefore, when the time was right for me, with God's help, I began to engage in activities that I previously enjoyed.

Well, my friends, thank you so much for taking this journey with me. I pray that you have been enlightened, encouraged, and reminded that although pain is so real, so is our gracious God. However, this is not the end of the book and you will want to discover the brief and interesting thoughts and stories that Donavan, family, and friends have to share about the influence of Justin's life and death.

> *"May the God of hope fill you with all joy and peace in believing [through the experience of your faith] that by the power of the Holy Spirit you will abound in hope and overflow with confidence in His promises."* (Romans 15:13, AMP)

Chapter 15

Justin's Answered Prayer (Leon Meets Vanessa)

A s shared in Chapter 8, Justin's desire was for me to meet someone who would be my companion for life. He was very particular about my well-being and such a romantic; therefore, he did not want me to live the rest of my life alone. Although I never shared my thoughts on this matter specifically with him, we were definitely on the same page. I did not want to be alone for the rest of my life.

Like so many single people of various ages, I attended Christian singles retreats, and the funny thing is, they were typically the equivalent of a Women's Retreat. In some cases, the ratio of women to men was like 100 to 1. Of course, the main reason a person should attend these functions is to be encouraged to be your best self as a single person, place your requests before God and trust His plan for your life. Even with that, reality stands up to say you at least want to be able to mingle with Christian single men.

I remember going through a brief period of time where I asked myself a very dangerous and derogatory question: "Is there something wrong with me?" This question is dangerous. It can create an incubator that grows a toxic focus on being in a dating relationship, which supersedes being happy in Christ and content with His plan for our lives. He loves us beyond measure and knows what's best for each of us.

As you can imagine though, I asked that derogatory question because instead of meeting my Boaz, the guys that I encountered were those who, for one reason or another, were not right for me and did not meet the specifics of my mantra: "I am fearfully and wonderfully made. The mark of God is upon me and I will not settle for anything or anyone less than I deserve, and I deserve the very best." The Holy Spirit inspired me to make a very freeing decision to live life with passion and embrace my singleness. The one thing that I feared more than being alone was being married to the person that God did not choose for me.

On July 9, 2015, I took my mantra a step further. I was listening to a Christian counselor who gave me a writing project. The assignment essentially encouraged imagining what your ideal marriage would look like and then writing out those thoughts. Ideally, this would be written as if you were already experiencing that relationship. I took the advice to heart and began to write about what I saw as my ideal relationship. I put it aside for several weeks and then began writing again, including every detail regarding my perception of a healthy marriage. I completed my assignment on July 21, 2015, put it aside, and didn't think of it again for almost an entire year.

In mid-June of 2016, one of my friends shared that there was a guy she wanted me to meet. Well, I don't know if you have ever had a well-meaning friend who introduced you to someone who made you wonder "How could you? What on earth were you thinking?" But that happened to me, which made me a little weary about meeting Leon. I asked lots of questions and discovered that his wife had passed away almost two years prior and that he was attractive and a good husband. So, I was convinced to at least meet the guy. Interestingly, later I discovered that he was hesitant about meeting me too for reasons similar to mine.

I'm not sure why I felt excited and flighty like a teenager about to go on a first date, but those were my emotions. So, I was so hyped about the idea of meeting and talking to Leon that when he called on June 10, 2016, I could not even answer the phone. I was in my car alone while verbally declaring, "I'm not ready... I'm not ready... I can't talk to him right now." So, do you know what I did? I let that call go to voicemail. Breathe... Inhale... Release.

Once I returned home, I gathered my thoughts and became calm enough to return Leon's call. To my delight, his deep, radio voice and conversation calmed all of my fears, and we talked on the phone for two hours. It was exciting to have these free-flowing conversations with this man who was a complete stranger just a few days prior. This pattern continued throughout the week as we headed toward the end of the week — the moment that we would meet.

That meeting was set to take place on Saturday at church, and I actually had butterflies. Once we had an opportunity to really talk after church though, the nervousness declined and our conversation continued to flow as it had during the week, as if we had known each other for years instead of days.

In fact, our first official date, outside of church, was a sunrise breakfast at the beach. Leon took the drive from North Carolina where he was living, which was about 90 minutes from where I live. He prepared everything, and my sole responsibility was to get in the car and buckle up. I had a sneaking suspicion that this was the beginning of more than just a car ride but the adventure of a lifetime. Once the car was unpacked, I was served various fruit and sparkling apple juice in glass goblets. The sunrise was beautiful, the weather perfect, and we practically had the beach all to ourselves. How's that for an accelerated first date?

When I think back, we had fun getting to know each other better as our relationship continued. It was beginning to feel more and more as if we had known each other since kindergarten. However, I couldn't help but also wonder, "Wait a minute. Do we need to pump the brakes?" After all, I did not want to make a regrettable decision. "Lord, if you don't choose Leon for me, I don't choose him either. If you say that he is the one, then I'm just going to tighten up my seatbelt and keep riding on this adventure." So, one day, I decided to say some of the things out loud that I had been saying to myself. "Do you know what Leon? I feel like we are moving too fast."

Leon's confident and calm response was "You're just afraid to admit how you really feel about me." At first, I just laughed when he said that. Then, I thought, "Hmmm. Is he right?" Am I afraid to make that commitment? Is it because I believe this is just too good to be true? That he is too good to be true? Had I become a student of the school of thought that says, "There are no good men left out there?"

Ironically, six months after our first conversation, Leon knelt on both knees and proposed. At that moment, I was taken by surprise. He tricked me! I really thought he was crawling around on the floor looking for something that he lost. I was clueless. Although it was December, it wasn't Christmas day, when I suspected this question might appear. So, by now, you know how my mind works. Ha! The neurons are silently firing! Do you remember the letter that I wrote about my ideal relationship and marriage? Well, shortly after we met, I began to wonder, "Where is that I letter? I believe there are several boxes that I could check off."

Finally, I found the letter and I was right! He met 98% of what I had written down. That's a pretty high score. There were a couple of items that had to remain unknown for now but everything else said, "This is my knight in shining armor." You can imagine, the silence was deafening for Leon as I processed my thoughts. So much so that he became almost fearfully certain that I would not accept his marriage proposal. My response was YES!

We set our wedding date for July 23, 2017, which is also Leon's birthday. He said this would be the best birthday gift he could have. This day that we had looked forward to, was not without challenges. It was almost time for the wedding to begin when a loud noise was heard: Boom! The power went out! All throughout the week, meteorologists were forecasting that very weekend to be the hottest weekend of the summer. Oh no! Lord, what were we going to do? Would we need to cancel our wedding?

As you can imagine, it was so very hot. My dear friends Patricia, who introduced Leon and I, and Tawanna were trying to help keep me reassured and hydrated. I could see inside the church and people were rapidly fanning. I expected people to start leaving, but I did not see anyone doing so. I spoke briefly with my fiancé, and he was ready to move forward. So much for superstition about seeing the bride before the wedding — Ha! We are prayerful but not superstitious.

Next, I saw the four mothers silently marching into the church. There was Leon's mother, my mother's best friend who is an adopted mother, Leon's mother-in-law from his late wife, and my mother-in-law from my late husband. Did I mention that my late husband's sister, Jackie, was my maid of honor? Yes, we were certainly graced with a unique set of mothers and remained close to our late spouses' families. Family is not just the lineage that you're born into but also those you choose. I could hear beautiful a cappella singing as they were marching, and yet, the voices reminded me that the piano was electric and there was no power.

Oh my! Then, the wedding director informed me it was time for Donavan and I to march in. "So, we are really going to do this in spite of the oven-like temperatures?" Yes, we are! My handsome son walked me down the aisle. He was closely followed by Justin's best friend, Richard. Why was Richard following behind? Ahhh... good question. Richard was there to represent Justin. He would have been so happy for me, and I could not think of getting married without him being represented. As we were marching down the aisle, there was more of that beautiful singing taking place. It was the voices of my talented new family, Vida and Portia, two of Leon's sisters, Fran and Renee, along with more of his sister-in-laws, nieces, and nephews from his previous marriage that were extending their melodic voices on our behalf to sing, "This Is My Prayer For You." I am told that I wore a beautiful smile and looked as though I was wrapped in the essence of serenity — as if I had not one care in the world. Look at God!

As we went through the ceremony, we could truly feel the presence of the Holy Spirit. This presence was especially evident as Pastor Anderson was beginning the marriage medley. He said, "This is your season for grace and favor!" At that moment, the lights and central air came back on! Boom! The power was restored, and everyone gave a loud cheer! As if that wasn't evidence enough of God's presence, Pastor Daryl Anderson personalized our marriage story by labeling us the Lion (Leon) and the Butterfly (Vanessa means butterfly). It was so beautiful.

After sealing our vows with a kiss, we marched down the aisle to a song that is considered very non-traditional for a wedding, and yet is very near and dear to our hearts. The song was "God Restores," written by Wayne Bucknor and made popular by a group called *Dynamic Praise*. It was the recessional song at Justin's funeral as I looked forward to the Resurrection and seeing my child again. It was the recessional song at our wedding as we looked forward to our future together as the Lion and the Butterfly.

> *"He escorts me to the banquet hall; it's obvious how much he loves me. Strengthen me with raisin cakes, refresh me with apples, for I am weak with love."* (Song of Songs 2:4-5, NLT)

Tributes to
Justin Emanuel Hanna

Young, Short-Lived, and Impactful

Grandma Dot

As I reflect on the relationship that my grandson and I experienced, a warm and fuzzy feeling surrounds me. Justin enjoyed visiting his grandparents' home in South Carolina. He enjoyed eating his Grandma's cooking, but on one such occasion, I burned the Stripples (vegetarian meat substitute).

He said, "Grandma, that's okay; they taste alright." But the next morning, he reminded me, "Grandma, don't burn the Stripples this morning!" We had a good laugh. At a later time, he was eating cornbread for lunch. He said, "Grandma, you cook the best cornbread in the world!"

Justin also had a spirit of sharing. We were returning home from a Pathfinders and Adventurers trip and as everyone got off the bus for a break, Justin passed and saw me; he asked, "Grandma, are you getting off?"

I replied, "No."

Justin pulled two dollars from his pocket and said, "Grandma, get something for you to drink."

As a teenager, Justin enjoyed helping me with house chores and yard work. He also assisted with grocery shopping. Once, while shopping at a grocery store that did not accept checks, my groceries had been totaled before I realized a personal check could not be used. I told Justin I would call my son, Justin's dad.

"No Grandma, I will pay for your groceries." And he did. He would not accept reimbursement. At that time, twenty-five dollars was a lot of money for a teenager. I was very grateful for his liberality and chose not to discourage his giving and sharing spirit.

When he had his next birthday, I asked Justin to give me a wish list, and he did. Of course, I added the money he had given his grandma and subsequently purchased the items he wished for on the list. He exclaimed to his mom, "Grandma hooked me up!"

When Justin attended Mount Pisgah Academy, he told his mother to bring Grandma with her. During this visit, he was very attentive and affectionate. As most teens do, Justin faced some challenges. But with God's help, he persevered. He loved his family and thoroughly enjoyed family celebrations. He showed deference and compassion toward the seniors and those who were less fortunate.

When he started attending Oakwood University, he called me one

morning and requested, "Grand-mommy, I want you to pray for me that I will be and stay focused."

He talked about his future life and the type of family he would like to have. However, his ultimate goal was to make it to heaven.

Yes, our hearts are broken over the passing away of our loved ones, but there is comfort and healing through prayer and God's Word. He is in control of everything; if we trust Him, He will work things out for our good.

Love, Grandma – Dorothy Mae McDuffie Hanna

Auntie Peaches (Jackie Hanna)

There are a few memories I love, but I think the one that we (the Hanna girls) talk about a lot is when Justin was 2 or 3 years old, and it was Christmas time. Auntie Nette bought him a cute outfit. You were trying to show him the outfit and you were making the appropriate "oohs and aahs" Justin's response was "I don't want it and I don't yike it," and threw it on the floor. I realized then that Justin was going to be his own person. Which, as he grew older, was good and also challenging at times for you all as parents, I'm sure.

I had the privilege of letting Justin and his best friend stay a week with me during their break while they were attending Oakwood. He seemed so young to be so mature. He had such plans... he thought so much about the future. Dreams/goals were vivid in his mind. During those conversations, I was amazed at how mature he had become.

He was our baby... he was so loving... I loved watching him grab his mom and kiss her ... I loved the way that he would hang out with his dad. Watching them, you could see how much they loved each other. He wasn't afraid or ashamed to show affection. He was who he was, and you could like it or not. He had a certain amount of ease moving about in this world that was comforting to watch. He had compassion for people. I remember my Mom telling me the story of how, when they were traveling on a bus on a Pathfinder trip and folks were getting off the bus to get snacks, he reached in his little pocket and said, "Here Grandma ... get something to drink." And throughout his short life, he would exhibit unselfishness in his own way. He had the courage to be himself.

He taught me that you don't have to be a certain age to be authentic.

He taught me that as long as you know who you are — that you could be comfortable handling yourself in situations others would balk at. He loved people and was not judgmental. He loved deeply. He loved his family. He believed in respecting his little girlfriend at the time and wasn't interested in being a "playa."

If he were here today, I would want him to keep God first, continue to love, continue to be authentic, and not let the experiences of life make him cynical.

This is very difficult — I love and miss my nephew, and this is very difficult!

Auntie Nette

ere it was... the perfect little Christmas outfit for my two-year-old nephew, Justin. Bubbling over with excitement, I placed the gift box in his little hands. He held the box and stared at it! I took the box and opened it, and after seeing the outfit Justin exclaimed, "I don't 'yike' it and I don't 'wont' it!" Of course, I was disappointed, but he was still "our baby."

Later as a college-age young man, I discovered that Justin had developed a style of his own, more of the trendy look. Because I am a "shopaholic," I enjoyed shopping for him and with him. The Thanksgiving prior to Justin's death, I took Justin and his friend, Richard, to the mall. What a blast we had shopping together. It was during this visit that I recognized Justin's love and acceptance of all people.

Auntie Margaret

Many of my memories and reflections of Justin were lived vicariously as various family members shared with me special moments about him. As my family and I relocated from one project to another, I anticipated telephone calls from family members with news of family happenings, especially with the nieces, nephews, and cousins.

During one of our summer vacations from Connecticut to South Carolina, we visited Granddad and Grandma Hanna. The visiting cousins ranged from 4 years old to pre-teen age. Justin's dad, Silvaris, played "Order My Steps" on the piano. As I write about this, images of Justin singing this song flash in my mind as he belted out the lyrics in his sweet, childlike voice, which could be heard above the rest. I believe this was a personal favor Justin asked of God because it was expressed in childlike faith. This childlike faith matured and blossomed in his relationship with others. One heart-warming experience I heard about was when Justin took off his new coat and gave it to a homeless man.

As I reminisce about one of the last interactions I had with Justin, I am reminded of how well-mannered, even-tempered, and insightful he was. Standing around the kitchen counter, he spoke of wanting to study political science to become a lawyer and become an effective agent in his community. His daily prayer was to have God order his steps.

Love, Auntie "M" – Margaret Ann Hanna Wright

Monique McCline

Thinking of Justin brings back so many memories. Too many to even know where to begin. A few of my favorite memories of him are always ones that bring a smile to my face. During an argument that I hate we had, Justin would always apologize and do what he could to change my mood. Whether he was right or wrong. He would do silly things, say something that caught me off guard, forcing me to smile, and reminded me that no matter what, he loved me dearly. Justin was always full of energy and laughter. That's another thing that will never fade in my memory — that big bright contagious smile and laugh. I smile every time I picture it.

What I loved most about Justin was his overall character, personality. I will never forget a time when there was this one kid who everybody was annoyed with, no matter if Justin was fond of him or not, he showed him love and kindness. He would laugh at his jokes, and if he ever saw him being treated as an outcast, he'd invite him to sit with us. I truly loved his kind spirit. I was proud to be his girlfriend, friend, and classmate. Always full of energy and always greeted everyone with a smile. Watching him was truly amazing and inspiring.

My family loved him, and vice versa. We video-chatted every chance we got, talked on the phone, wrote letters. When I got that tragic call, I was devastated. I didn't believe it for one second, but then I realized something was truly wrong when I noticed he never responded, when he always did. So, I guess I knew before I was told, but I prayed my hardest for it to not be true. Justin truly felt like my other half, and his death impacted me terribly. I turned from God – didn't want to hear anything about Him. I was listening to a voicemail of Justin's he had left me. He had said towards the end, "Remember to always pray, babe, no matter how unfair things may seem." So, I did. Immediately I felt this feeling of comfort; it actually felt like there was someone hugging me. His death has reminded me of the true healing power that God is capable of. His love and mercy.

Spending the time that I did with Justin has taught me many things, such as what it means to have true chemistry with someone. How to have boundaries and stick to them, to appreciate every moment you have with the person you love, whether it's just your friend, family, or significant other. I've learned to not take those small arguments so seriously and to always say, "I'm sorry; I love you," before laying down. Going that extra mile for a stranger does more for you than it does them. When you know what you want, go for it and don't let anybody stop you, or tell you differently. If he were here today, we probably would've gotten married.

If he were here today, I'd tell him "I love you, and thank you for being that positive role model in my life."

All in all, I have learned so much from him. There are still a lot of tears as well as joy. Justin was the most kind, courageous, determined, smart, witty, stylish person I have ever met. Never was afraid to be different; he embraced it. I'm glad he has touched and impacted so many other people and not just me. I will always cherish the moments I had with him.

Love, Monique McCline, girlfriend

Richard Lawerence

Through Loss, I Truly Found Christ

You never truly know what tomorrow brings; life is interesting in that manner. In this life, certain experiences fulfill the yearnings of our basic needs as people. I believe friendship is one of those experiences for most, and it truly is an experience. I'm referring to true friendship, not casual acquaintances, classmates, or coworkers we schmooze within certain seasons of our lives before we leave that job or graduate from that institution.

I mean true friendship, described as "iron sharpening iron," and "loveth at all times." This experience is a privilege that not all partake of in this life. If you're an exception, you ought to count it a blessing as I have. For myself, Justin Emanuel Hanna was that experience. His genuine personality was a rarity; we were closer than most brothers. He was just a trustworthy guy with a heart of gold, who cared deeply for his family and friends. And if you were his friend, you might as well have been family. Some of my favorite memories of us are things that still make me smile when life starts to do what it does best. He was really something special, and I consider it a blessing to have experienced that sort of bond in this life. I've recently decided that my son will have his name, and the tip of that legacy will be until that wonderful day when he and I are back at it.

Love, Richard Lawerence, friend and brother

Verses to Remember

"These things I have spoken to you, that in me you may have peace. In the world you will have tribulation; but be of good cheer, for I have overcome the world." (John 16:33, NKJV)

"Therefore you now have sorrow; but I will see you again and your heart will rejoice, and your joy no one will take from you." (John 16:22, NKJV)

Antonio McFadden

There are many things I can say about Justin Emanuel Hanna. One of those things: He was a gentle giant. Every moment Justin and I shared made me respect and revere him so much. His presence was that of a strong, stocky man, but his heart was that of a loving and caring person.

There are so many memories that I could talk about regarding Justin. One memory that sticks out when I reflect on Justin is the memory of our clothing venture we wanted to start together! Both of us being men of fashion and loving nice clothes, we decided to start sketching our own men's apparel.

There are many other memories of Justin and myself switching majors together, but perhaps the most memorable moment in our friendship is the moment when he asked me to sing at his funeral! It was late one night, and he and I were both up singing, but out of the blue Justin mysteriously says, "I want you to sing at my wedding or if I die before you, I want you to sing at my funeral," and I'm looking at him like "You are crazy!" I'll probably die before you, but indeed, in March 2012, I would have the humbling responsibility to sing at my brother's funeral.

The legacy that Justin has left behind for me would be, that even in death, he still was a gentle giant! His love and compassion for those who knew him rang throughout the halls of OU for a long time after he left us. He will never be forgotten!

If Justin were here today, I would say to him "Thank you!" Thank you for the lessons you've taught us even in your death. Justin will never leave our hearts!

Love, Antonio McFadden, friend

Emmanuel Winston

To think of Justin is to think of the fun times. I remember the times when we stayed over at my house or his house, and it was always fun. As kids, we played video games all night or would run to the gas station for junk to eat. Also, we always enjoyed going to see Auntie Doris at the church school or at grandma's house.

There are so many wonderful memories to cherish. With laughter, I recall one summer, we worked in sister Scott's yard, cleaning it to help make a little money as kids. That was some of the hardest work we had ever done. We knew at the end of that summer we never wanted to clean yards again! Justin and I always had fun, even at church.

As I think back, our conversations are even more cherished now than they were. Justin and I would talk about going to Mount Pisgah Academy, as we would take a trip with his mom or brother to see the school and friends. We both wanted to go to this school, but I also tried a few times to get Justin to come to Wilson back home in Florence. However, he had his heart set on Mount Pisgah. I have to admit it though, I enjoyed the weekend trips I would take with Aunt Nessa to see Justin at school.

Little did we know Justin would end up going to Wilson for a brief period – the year after I graduated. However, it still felt good knowing your little brother was at your alma mater. Sometimes I find myself just wishing I could pick up the phone to call Justin to just have a talk with him about life. I miss just checking in on my brother.

Justin always had a big heart and was willing to help everybody any way he could. I recall he began working out big time at Oakwood. He got a little more muscle on him as he started college and became his own MR. GQ. His enhanced physique made our wrestling matches much more challenging!

Other fun memories include the times when we would stay up late on some nights at his house and wake up super early to ask uncle Don to take us to the YMCA to play basketball. Other times, we would go out front and play with his dad two-on-one. We always made the best of all the times we have had with each other.

Sadly, he never had a chance to meet my kids, but I know they would have loved Uncle Justin. I tell them about Uncle Justin and show them his picture on the wall. I've often said to my wife, "If we ever have a second son, I would like him to be named Justin." Actually, we share the name Emanuel. Although we have slightly different spellings, it is still pronounced the same. Emanuel was his middle name and Emmanuel is my first name.

Obviously, Justin was more than just a cousin to me; he was more like a brother. I miss my brother.

Love, Emmanuel Winston, cousin and brother

Salisha Rigsbee

How would you describe Justin? Justin was always full of life, always willing to try stunts and push the envelope. He wasn't afraid of danger. Favorite memories? Sitting at church one night and discussing going to law school. My best friend Chelsey was supposed to be keeping a secret about me trying to get into law school, but somehow told Justin, lol. So Justin walks up to me and says, "So how is the process to go to law school going?" Chelsey's face dropped and she stared at him as if that was their secret. We all ended up laughing about it and he went right into telling me about his dreams of going to law school, but not any law school. He specifically said he would be going to Harvard. His confidence was always so contagious. Loved the way he owned who he was. That night, I left a little more secure in who I was and went harder in the process to go to law school.

What did you learn from him? I learned that a simple conversation with someone can change the way you view something.

What legacy did he leave? For me personally, he left inspiration. I went through law school with his photo on my laptop every single day. I was reminded that I am here with an opportunity and that no matter how hard it was, I had to keep pushing. Looking at the photo, I knew that he was rooting for me, I knew that he was studying with me, that he was right beside me every step of the way. He left a piece of himself with me just by being genuine. His spirit pushed me every step of the way.

If he was here today what would you say to him? Not quite sure; I'd probably be sharing law school horror stories with him and discussing the issues within our government. But to his absence I say, thank you for being who you were. Thank you for the time you gave us. Thank you for always greeting me with a smile and a hug while smelling so good lol. Thank you for your friendship and thank you for the hope you left me with. You will always be loved.

Love, Attorney Salisha Rigsbee, friend

Chelsey Richardson

There are some people that are easy to forget. Then there are people like Justin, a smile, a spirit, a soul I will never forget. I knew Justin from the time he was a little boy, but I got to know him more in his teenage years. I had the opportunity to tutor Justin during his high school years. While I was supposed to be teaching him, he taught me more than he may have ever known.

Justin lived without fear. He was literally a daredevil. I remember the excitement in his eyes and in his voice when I would come over to tutor him, and he'd say "Yo, check out this video I made today. I jumped off the roof of the house". Because he could do anything, apparently, he thought anyone could. Justin would have me (overweight and all) jumping over tables, trying to do handstands, and frog poses. Being such a great acrobat, Justin genuinely believed anything was possible and his belief was so contagious. I often think about where I am today and how I would love to share those moments with him. Not only to share those moments with him, but to thank him for the way he lived his life. Justin taught me to live free and give freely. His smile, his spirit, and his soul will forever rest with me. Until we meet again, I will be working on my frog poses and handstands. I know that he would be proud.

Love, Chelsey Richardson, friend

Vanessa Lawerence

When the news of Justin's death was shared with me, I was devastated. At that time, so many feelings and emotions were experienced. Disbelief, numbness, sorrow, helplessness, suffering, and anguish to name a few were at the doorpost of my heart. I couldn't believe this was happening.

As a mother, it impacted me in a way I really cannot fully express. I still have difficulty talking to Richard about our feelings. We really don't talk about it. That chapter in our life is essentially like an open file with no full closure. However, I've learned to embrace every moment with my children, family, and friends because time is not promised to any of us. It's essentially borrowed and numbered. I sometimes think about how things would have been. Like, graduation and how the two of them would have been there to have a celebration together. Marriage — who Justin would have chosen? I know if he were living, he would have been Richard's best man. Sometimes I'm sad because I feel guilty that you (Vanessa Hanna-Verrett) suffered such loss, and I'm still enjoying Richard's growth in life. It's tearful — makes me very sad.

But I'm very happy about the relationship that has taken place between you and Richard. I've never said it, but he really has two mothers. If anything happens to me and you are alive, I hope you'll continue to provide him with the motherly comfort and love you've given. That's how I view life now. Love, share, and embrace the moments with family and friends.

Love, Vanessa Lawrence, sister, friend

Michael Brackett

Pablo Picasso once recounted, "My mother said to me, 'If you are a soldier, you will become a general. If you are a monk, you will become the Pope.' Instead, I was a painter, and became Picasso."

Vanessa Hanna-Verrett had a son in whom she saw much promise. A son showing the kind of qualities that could help him become a strong and successful man. Vanessa Hanna-Verrett inspired her son, Justin, for greatness – by pointing him to a Power not from within, but from above. The kind of Power that can help a man live a more vibrant life than even the great Picasso.

I had the privilege to know Justin Hanna as his high school academy chaplain. Quiet and strong, it was a pleasure to watch his growth from a boy into a fine young man. There was an inner confidence that was his, and I knew it was aided by a devout and praying mother.

In college, Justin would call his mother daily so they could both share devotional time with the Source of their strength — God. Together, they grew stronger, claiming the assurance and promises that come from being children of God and heirs of His eternal kingdom.

Justin will one day soon rise again. He will be strong and successful. He will never again be separated from Vanessa, because with God, if you are a sinner, you are forgiven. With God, if you are forgiven, you are a saint. With God, if you are a saint, you have broken free from the chains of this world and will enjoy a masterpiece of existence, painted on the most colorful tapestry of eternity by the God of love.

Chaplain Michael Brackett, previously Associate Pastor at Mount Pisgah Academy, during Justin's enrollment. Currently, chaplain in the Oregon Conference of Seventh Day Adventists.

Sources

*https://www.forbes.com/sites/jackzenger/2018/04/08/the-confidence-gap-in-men-and-women-why-it-matters-and-how-to-overcome-it/#1d795baa3bfa.

Cousins, N. (2011). *The Remarkable Story of Norman Cousins - Laugh Off Life.* Laugh Off Life. https://sites.google.com/site/laughofflife/page-1.

Laughter Therapy as Stress Relief. Skills You Need. (2017). https://www.skillsyouneed.com/ps/therapeutic-laughter.html.

Mason, I. (2013, October 15). *Laughing away pain.* Medical News Today. https://www.medicalnewstoday.com/articles/267434.

Mayo Clinic Staff. (2020). *Stress relief from laughter? It's no joke.* MayoClinic. https://www.mayoclinic.org/healthy-lifestyle/stress-management/in-depth/stress-relief/art-20044456.

About the Author

Born and raised in Florence, SC Vanessa Hanna-Verrett earned a BA degree in Business Administration from Francis Marion University. Her passion for coaching those who have suffered loss is one that drives her. Alongside her husband Leon, Vanessa co-facilitates grief support meetings for the community through her church in South Carolina. She and her husband are also the creators of the podcast, The Struggle Is Real In Grief which is available on Itunes, Spotify, Google and other platforms.

Vanessa draws from her purposeful life story when writing about the experiences of losing a husband and a son 3-years apart in her debut book Pursuing Hope: The Story of Justin Hanna. Through her reflections about parental love, unimaginable loss and the pursuit of hope and restoration Vanessa hopes that readers will increase in faith and trust the healing process. Vanessa has Completed Grief Recovery Facilitator training and currently enrolled in Dr. H. Norman Wright's Grief, Center. She currently supports military survivors in a Tragedy Assistance Program.

www.verrettministry.com

CPSIA information can be obtained
at www.ICGtesting.com
Printed in the USA
BVHW031956280622
640649BV00005B/12

9 781948 877695